LINUX
COMMAND LINE

*A Practical Guide
Beyond the Basics*

TRAVIS BOOTH

TABLE OF CONTENTS

iii

Preface

———•◆•———

Linux Operating system, with its many distributions, is the foremost and flexible operating system worldwide. Linux operating system is utilized in several spaces in the field of Computer Science, stretching from home appliances to industrial machines running countless platforms driving industry. This operating system has found uses in Artificial Intelligence, Parallel computing, also known as High-Performance Computing, Cloud Computing, all the powerful Data Centre infrastructures that are powering the global internet infrastructure services like DNS, Content Delivery Networks and Digital Security.

The Linux Operating System is issued with native and contemporary graphical user interfaces that are tailored to the distribution of Linux in use ranging from GNOME to KDE to Cinnamon. On any Linux computer, the command line or command-line interface abbreviated CLI is the most authoritative and elastic way of cooperating with the Linux kernel and helper services. A Linux command-line interface or CLI is used to execute specific commands. In Linux Operating systems, a command is a set of instructions sent to the Linux kernel to tell the Computing device what to do. The Linux command line can also execute and interpret commands from a written text file called a bash, python, and other scripts, which enables easy automation of tasks.

Many System administration tasks are routine and repetitive that need to be automated, for example, automatically like sending alerts, e-mails, and performing routine maintenance. This book contains beginner information about the Linux command line, shell, and bash scripting. The book introduces the novice Linux user to basic Linux scripting skills to automate and perform several sys-admin tasks. These range from parsing text and interpreting it to the automation of network services operations. Linux is a fantastic tool for automation and it's all done via the Linux command-line tool.

What this Book Covers

This book is a follow up to "The Linux Command Line – Getting started with Bash and Shell Scripting" book, which was an immersive introduction into the Linux Operating system bash shell, how to configure the shell and the Linux environment and writing basic command-line shell scripts. This Intermediate Command-Line book will be an extension of the previous book in this series. The book will detail Linux Process Management, Linux Networking, and Perl Scripting in the command line. The book will end with Automating using Ansible.

Chapter 1: The first chapter will be a review of the basic command line concepts covered in the Linux Command Line book. This chapter will cover Linux File System, navigation and directory basics, command redirection, file searching, and basic scripting, as covered in the first book in the series.

Chapter 2: this chapter will be an in-depth look at the Linux file system, Redirection, and more advanced concepts of pipelining.

Chapter 3: this chapter will introduce Linux File system Permissions, looking at the reading, writing, and execution permissions. We will detail chmod, su, sudo and umask commands

Chapter 4: this chapter will look at VI preview from the first book in the series and the advanced concepts of the VI editor.

Chapter 5: this chapter is a detailed look at Processes in Linux, deep-diving into viewing, controlling, signals, and commands used with Linux Processes.

Introduction

———◆———

This is an Intermediate Linux Command Line book, which is the second installment in the three-book Linux Command Line series. The first book in the series is called "The Linux Command Line – Getting started with Bash and Shell scripting." This book covered the fundamentals of what an Operating System and then introduced the reader to the world of the Linux operating system. The first book in the series then went on to introduce the command line and all the concepts surrounding this immensely critical component of the Linux operating system.

This second installment of the Linux Command Line series will begin by doing a review of the fundamental concepts covered in the first book like Linux Operating System and why people use the Operating System over other proprietary systems. In this introductory section, we will start by reviewing what an Operating system is. We will then further detail the functions of an operating system, before briefly introducing the reader to Linux.

Operating System (OS)

An operating system is a computer hardware and software management program for users. Originally, operating systems were built to conduct repetitive hardware duties that focused on file management, running programs, and receiving user instructions. Using a user interface, you communicate with an operating system's kernel that enables the operating system to obtain and interpret user-sent instructions. To execute a job, you only need to submit an instruction to the operating system, such as reading a file or printing a document, and the operating system will coordinate with the hardware to execute that instruction.

Functions of the OS

Operating systems have several functions and purposes, but the primary purpose is to provide an interface between a User and the computer hardware. Below we have the detail about different functions that the operating system performs. The operating system has the following functions;

Resource Manager

The Linux Operating System, like any other OS, is a Resource Manager. This means that it manages all hardware resources that are attached to the system, such as Memory and Central Processing Unit and all Input Devices. The operating system will determine when the CPU will perform which operation.

Process Manager

The operating system is always monitoring and observing processes that are concurrently running on your machine. The OS keeps track of various executing tasks and chooses which process will use the CPU and when it has access to the CPU. The operating system provides procedures to start, stop, and change process states.

Hardware Manager

When the Linux Operating System initializes through a process called boot process, the system performs a process called POST which stands for Power On Self-Test; which is a process through which the OS and computer discover all the system hardware components currently attached to the Computer (CPU, hard drive, USB devices, and network cards) and loads the device drivers and modules required to access those particular hardware devices.

Memory Manager

Memory management is the function where the operating system handles and manages the primary memory and extended memory of the Computer System. Memory management entails movement of system and custom processes back and forth between the main memory and the secondary memory during execution, such as the hard drive. Memory management also keeps track of all volatile memory places on the computer, irrespective of whether they are freely assigned to some processor. This operator finds out the quantity of memory to be assigned to specific procedures. Applications in Linux require RAM (random access memory) and swap space (extended memory) to function. The operating system is responsible for memory management to ensure optimal sharing of this resource by various programs running on the system.

File System Manager

File system constructs or components are either built-in into the Linux operating system or loaded as modules. In Linux, everything is viewed as a file from directories, processes, and devices. The Linux operating system plays a significant part in controlling who owns and who has access to processes, files, and folders, also known as directories that the file systems contain.

User and Group Manager

System Administrators in all major operating systems add, update, delete, and manage user and group accounts on their systems. The Linux operating system facilitates the addition, deletion, and updating of user and group accounts and managing related user and group access permissions and level of control a user has on the system. Individual users and group accounts in Linux facilitate user access to their files and processes they own or are owned by other users of the System.

Programming Tools

The Linux operating system offers several programming tools for developing programs and libraries to implement Application Programming Interfaces that allow Linux to connect with many other Programs.

What is Linux?

Linux is a robust, lightweight, and secure open-source operating system that has enterprise-level Internet services, extensive development tools, fully functional graphical user interfaces (GUIs), and a massive number of applications ranging from office suites to multimedia applications (Petersen, 2008).

Linux is one of the twenty-first century's most outstanding technological advances. In addition to its effect on massive Internet growth and its position as an enabling technology for a range of computer-driven systems, Linux development has been a model of how cooperative initiatives can surpass what people and businesses can do alone (Negus, 2015).

Linux operating system, like any other operating system, is composed of the Kernel, GNU utilities, a graphical user interface (GUI), and application programs. The detailed components above each play a crucial role in the Linux operating system's functions.

The Linux Kernel

The Linux operating system's core component also referred to as its heart, is the kernel. The kernel regulates all computer system hardware and software, allocating hardware if needed, and implementing software if required. The kernel is mainly accountable for four primary tasks, namely the management of system memory, software program management, hardware management, and file system management.

As an operating system, Linux comprises of the kernel and its components that oversee the management of your software and hardware and allows you to run application programs on your System.

Chapter 1

Linux CLI Review

---◆---

In this first chapter, we are going to review the fundamental Linux and command line concepts covered in the first book in this series, "The Linux Command Line." We are going to concentrate on the Bash shell and its environment. We will have a brief introduction into the command line Interpreter, Shell, and Bash. We will guide the user on how to write their first Bash script.

Command-line Structure

The Linux command line is a text-based user interface on your server that is utilized by the system user to interact with software and hardware of your machine; this interface takes user-entered commands or instructions interprets them and return an output. Frequently denoted as the shell, terminal, console, prompt, or many additional titles.

The Linux command line is the most central means to interact with a Linux system. That is, the command line is the interface between a computer user and the Linux Operating System's kernel and computing hardware. The shell prompt ending with $ or # for user root indicates that it is ready for user input.

You can access the Linux Shell by Pressing Ctrl+Alt+F1 or F2 or F3 or F4 or F5 or F6 when you are logged in on the Graphical User

Interface. These commands open up a shell terminal where commands can be entered to give your software and hardware user instructions. The Linux terminal runs a shell, which is a programming environment that can be used to perform automated tasks. Shell programs are termed bash scripts. The table below is a listing of the standard and regular shells in the Linux operating system:

Typical Linux Shells	
The Bourne shell	/bin/sh
The Bourne again shell	/bin/bash
The Korn shell	/bin/ksh
The C shell	/bin/csh
Tom's C shell	/bin/tcsh

Since the bash shell is one of the most widely used shells, we shall concentrate on the use of bash in Linux. We are going to review various Linux commands to perform basic file management commands in the Linux System. In this section of the book, we will introduce the reader to the Linux Command Structure looking at the variables and inherent command options, the Interactive Shell, metacharacters, and quotes plus perform the following:

- Carry out Basic File Management Operations including creating, Deleting, Editing, Renaming, Copying, etc. file contents and folders

- Moving around the file system;

- Find files and directories; and.

- Work with hard and soft links.

The Command Line

Users can access Linux operating system through the Graphical User Interface, also known as the GUI and through the command line interface, also known as the CLI. The command-line interface, also referred to as the shell, the terminal, or console, is Linux's text-based interface through which users send instructions to the operating system and the hardware. The instructions in the Linux OS are sent through entering commands, which are instructions to your computer in the shell terminal. Every command has one or more options and one or more arguments. The CLI (command-line interface) reads and interprets shell commands; If you use the KDE or Gnome GUI, you open a terminal emulator to access the CLI. If you access your computer's text-based login, you will see the CLI as a BASH shell.

The Linux Shell

The shell has an essential function in a Linux operating system – running commands. The shell is nothing more than a program, designed to read commands a user enters via the keyboard. It then passes the commands to a kernel so they can be processed or executed. You could consider the shell as program language, with variables, functions, arrays and other data structure. It has a direct connection to the shell, which means it has file i/o primitives already in the syntax.

11

It allows interactive access, both the kernel and to any program on it. The shell will function as a standard program, executing code, starting when a user has logged in. It could also be seen as a macro processor, interpreting user instructions and executing them, by way of keyboard-entered user commands.

The shell also bash commands to be executed, both synchronously and asynchronously. It waits for a command to finish before it will take any more input – while it reads extra commands and executes them, asynchronous commands carry on performing. The redirection constructs allow strong control over the inputs and the outputs. The shell also allows users to control command setting content and provides a few commands, built-in, that may not gain functionality via certain services. A user may check the types of shells **/etc/shells** that their system accepts:

```
[ppeters@rad-srv ~]$ cat /etc/shells
/bin/bash
/bin/sh
/sbin/nologin
/bin/dash
/bin/tcsh
/bin/csh
```

Every user created on the Linux system has a default shell set for them. The default shell settings are kept in the **/etc/passwd** file. Below is an example**/etc/passwd** entry for user *ppeters*:

```
ppeters:x:500:500::/home/ppeters:/bin/bash
```

Linux File System

At the center of any Linux OS is the Linux Kernel. The Linux Kernel is the principal part or heart of the operating system and delivers the facility for software to access the computer hardware. The kernel functions via files, as do most other systems and applications that run on Linux. Pretty much every way that an operating system interacts with applications, users and security models depends on how files are stored. It is crucial that, for many reasons, programs and users can refer to a set of standard guidelines to know how and where files should be read and written.

The table below summarizes a logical arrangement of files within the Linux Operating System:

	Shareable These are files that are not available to other hosts	Unshareable These are files that are accessible by various hosts
Variable These are files that can change at any time without intervention	/var/mail /var/spool/news /home	/var/run /var/lock /tmp
Static These are files that do not change without an intervention from the system administrator	/usr /opt	/etc /boot

The reason why we look at files in this approach is to aid in linking the function of the file with the requisite permissions assigned to the directories which hold the files. How the operating system and its users interact with a given file determines the directory in which it is placed, whether that directory is mounted read-only or read-write, and the level of access each user has to that file. The top level of this structure is crucial, as the access to the underlying directories can be restricted, or security problems may manifest themselves if the top level is left disorganized or without a widely used structure.

To achieve this, many Linux operating systems ascribe to the FHS, also called the file system hierarchy standard. FHS is a Linux filesystem standard that describes the designations and places that files and folders should take. Filesystems are expected to conform to FHS standard since it guarantees compatibility with systems that also conform to the Standard.

The root folder /

The Linux file system's root folder is the main folder in Linux, the filesystem that holds other files and directories. The folder is named the root folder because it's at the edge of the inverted tree-like hierarchical file structure. The folder is used to manage every other subfolder and files on the filesystem.

The root directory for Linux is a fundamental unit of the entire file system. When a system boots up, the initial section to be started is the root or main directory. This directory contains the elements needed to bring the machine to life. The root folder contains

14

system booting information and most Linux application utilities required for system configuration. Additionally, both Linux applications that are needed to install external file systems are contained in the root directory. These tools may include networking devices, for example, in an interconnected environment, since mounts can be rendered can NFS. Last but not least, the software to patch faulty file systems and produce a restoration for system crashes are also found in the root directory.

Under different conditions, the system administrator's purpose is to preserve the root directory as possible at the smallest size. The smaller the maintained filesystem is, the less likely it is to be compromised once there is a crash of the system. The root fs is a database for vital Linux resources or applications with significant settings kept in the /etc. directories. This ensures that the root fs is not shared. We can minimize the size of storage space needed if we maintain a small root filesystem, especially in places with slow connectivity.

/boot folder
The Linux/boot folder includes items necessary for the initial phase of the Linux boot cycle. This folder holds the required data before even the kernel starts running user applications. We have a backup of all boot documents, boot sector location files, and several other things that don't need manual updating.

/dev folder
This /dev/ folder comprises hardware device entries which represent peripherals connected to the computer system. These device files are crucial to the smooth system functioning.

/etc. folder

In Linux, we have the folder /etc/ which is used to store and be a database for all local system configuration files. The /etc/ folder doesn't hold binary files. In Linux, all the configuration or setting files are merely ordinary files that assist in managing the functioning of all Linux processes and programs.

/lib/ folder

We have libraries in Linux, like in any other operating system. The /lib/ folder is a repository for these libraries required to execute or run binary files which are stored /bin/ folder and /sbin/ directory. Libraries kept in this folder are especially vital at system startup and for processing programs in the root filesystem.

/mnt/ folder

The Linux filesystem /mnt/ folder is meant for the provisional setup of filesystems in portions of the disk named mount points. The /mnt/ folder is used to mount DVDRoms and USB disks. The process of linking an external special file system, which is on DVD-ROMs, hard disk drives, and other storage resources to the already available and accessible computer file system, is called mounting. This process means mark out a part of the file system to open special files.

/opt/ folder

The folder /opt/ provides space for big, defined packages of computer programs. A program in the folder /opt/ which holds the data creates a folder with the same title as the item. This folder, in effect, contains files that would then be directed into the file system, providing the system manager with a simple means of establishing that file's purpose within a particular set.

/proc/ folder

The folder called the /proc/ consists of special files that either obtain data from just the kernel or transmit it to the same kernel. This folder may also be employed to interact with the kernel given the wide range of data currently inside /proc/ and its many forms.

/sbin/ folder

The system's superuser only employs the filesystem /sbin/ folder for executable files. The executable files kept in the /sbin/ are mainly used for system booting and mounting /usr/ folder and performing system restoration activities.

/usr/ folder

The Linux filesystem's folder called /usr/ is an incredibly important file containing that contains custom binaries, their libraries and documentation files, libraries, and header files that can be shared by all users connected to the system. The root user can only write this folder. This folder is a file that can be shared with read-only permissions. The / usr / directory usually has its own partition, and this should be the case.

The /var/ Directory

The /var directory is a shared directory that stores temporary files and folders. All logged, locked, spooled, and cached files are appropriately stored under subdirectories in /var. Since the FHS requires Linux to mount /usr/ read-only, any programs that write log files or need spool/ or lock/ directories should be written to the /var/ directory.

The Interactive Shell

The syntax of shell commands is displayed below:

[ppeters@rad-srv ~]$ command [options] {arguments}.

To print text to the screen, the bash shell will use the **echo command.**

[ppeters@rad-srv ~]$ echo "introduction to echo."

The Linux shell extrapolates that the first word in any given statement or string typed or entered on the terminal is the command. If the string is a full or relative path to an executable, then that executable or binary on the said path is started. If the first word has no forward slash symbol (/), then the shell will scan directories defined in the PATH variable and attempt to run the first command matching that string.

For instance, if the PATH variable only contains the directories **/bin** and **/usr/bin,** then a command saved in the folder **/etc.** will be inaccessible; hence, it is important to specify the full path.

Alternatively, a relative path may be used. For example, if a specific program is stored in the current working directory, a user could type:

[ppeters@rad-srv ~]$ ./<Program Name>

Variables in Shell

In Linux bash scripting, we have variables that are akin to variables or parameters used in other computing languages. Names of parameters or variables in Linux shell are limited to alphanumeric letters and numbers. SALARY=1300, for instance, basically sets the 1300 value to the SALARY parameter.

Initializing a bash variable:	name_of_variable=value
Referencing a bash variable:	$name_of_variable

Example:

[ppeters@rad-srv ~]$ SALARY=1400
[ppeters@rad-srv ~]$ echo $SALARY
1400
[ppeters@rad-srv ~]$

File System Navigation

In the Linux environment, everything is regarded as a file starting with folders, actual regular files, system programs, system, and regular processes and devices. The most principal and critical command-line purposes are traversing the Linux OS file and directory makeup. There a numerous inbuilt bash shell utilities or commands utilized to navigate across a Linux folder. All Linux OS variants use the Hierarchical File Structure that begins at the Linux file system root directory (/) moving down to files or subdirectories. We principally have three foremost commands used for file or folder navigation namely:

- **pwd**: This word represents the full statement Print Working Directory. This shell command displays the folder on the filesystem that the user is currently in.

```
[root@rad-srv ~]# pwd
/root
```

- **cd:** CD is a command to move or jump from one directory to the next. CD Stands for Change Directory.

```
[root@rad-srv ~]# cd /var/log
[root@rad-srv log]#
```

- **ls**: The ls command is used to display the contents of a directory.

```
[root@rad-srv sysconfig]# ls
anaconda console grub kdump network rdisc rsyslog snmptrapd
sysstat.ioconf atd  cpupower     init
```

Listing Directory Contents

To list the files and directories in the current working directory, we use the **ls** command.

```
[ppeters@rad-srv ~]$ ls
```

```
Desktop Documents Music Pictures Public Templates Videos
```

Introduction to Directories

A directory is a file whose major function is to store file names and their related details. Directories or Folders in Linux, whether they are ordinary, special, or directory, contain all files.

Linux operating system uses the hierarchical structure to organize files and directories. The Directory tree is the name given to this structure in Linux. The directory tree starts with the single root node, the slash character (/), and every other folder falls under the root directory.

Linux operating system has three basic types of files, namely regular, directories, and special files. **Regular Files** are those files that contain text, data, or program code/scripts. **Directories** are a type of file, also called folders that contain or store both special and regular files. Linux directories are the exact equivalent to folders in Windows. We also have what are called **Special Files** in Linux. These special files give us access to several hardware devices such as hard drives, keyboards, monitors, CD-ROM drives, USB flash devices, and Ethernet adapters.

Listing Files in Directories

System administrators in Linux do a lot of troubleshooting and use several tools. We have a tool to display a list of folders and the files stored in the current directory, and we use the ls (listing) command:

```
[ppeters@rad-srv ~]$ ls
```

This ls command is used with several options such as the **-l** option which gives more details about the listed files:

```
[ppeters@rad-srv ~]$ ls -l
total 8578999
drwxrwxr-x        2 ppeters        ppeters 4698  Sept 2 09:59
-rw-rw-r--    1 ppeters    ppeters 45371 Sept 2 08:38 12.jpg
drwxr-xr-x        2 ppeters        ppeters 5659        Sept    1
2019folder1
drwxr-xr-x        2 root        root        4096   Sept    1
2019folder2
[ppeters@rad-srv ~]$
```

The ls –l command gives us the long listing of the contents of the file or directory. The ls –l command displays more information, and we are going to break it down. **The first character** to the far left represents the type of the file. Reading from the output above, we have character **d,** which represents a directory and – (hyphen) represents a regular file. Just next to the first character in the output, we have the File Permissions column. There are nine characters in this column broken down into 3by3 fields, which represent user, group, and global file permissions. The nine characters are broken down into three character batches with each three character batch having read, write and execute permissions. In the output above, the first **rwx** represents read, write and execute permissions assigned to the owner of the file. The second **r-x** for folder 1 means that group ppeters has read and execute permissions, but no write permissions to folder1.

The next or second column in the output is the Number of Links field. For folder1, there are two links. The third column or field displays the owner of the displayed file. In our example above, the owner is ppeters. The fourth column is a display of the group to which the owner of the file belongs to. The fifth field is the Size column. This column specifies the size of the file in bytes. The sixth field or column is the **Last modified date & time. This field** specifies the date and time of the last modifications done to the file. The last column is the name of the file.

The output of the ls –l command shows the type of the file in the first character of the output result. From the example above, we have – and the d characters — the table below details all the types of files that we have in Linux and their associated symbols.

Number	Symbol and its explanation
1	- Ordinary file, such as a text file, binary file, or hard link.
2	**B** Special Block file representing a Block I/O device file such as a hard drive.
3	**C** Special Character file representing a raw file such as a physical hard drive.
4	**D** Represents a Directory file that displays a list of contained files and directories.
5	**L** This symbol represents a soft or Symbolic link file. These are Links on any ordinary file.
6	**P** This symbol represents named pipe. This is a mechanism for inter-process communications.
7	**s** This symbol is for Sockets used in inter-process communication.

Bash Input/Output Redirection

Redirection is the process of capturing output from a text file in the command line designated as the script file, from a regular command, and lastly, from a regular file.

Redirection is performed through the use of some expressions, which are regular or wild card symbols. To redirect output into an ordinary **file,** we employ Linux shell meta character called angle **brackets** '<,">', or to capture output to a **program we use** the shell meta character called the **pipe** symbol '|.'

When the bash shell commands are processed, there is continuous input or output redirection through evaluation and understanding of special notations. Redirections enable the FD or file descriptors of the bash commands to open and close. Through redirections, file descriptors refer to various files and may change files from which we read the commands. Redirections in current bash shell processing settings are used to change file descriptors. Input and output redirections process from left to right in the order they appear.

Whenever you see the redirection statement with the **less than operator sign** "<" and no file descriptor number, know that we are referring to the standard input (file descriptor 0). Whenever we use the **greater than sign** ">" and the file handler number is omitted, then we are referring standard output (file descriptor 1).

Standard Output

Bash command-line interface, also known as the terminal, has built-in result console called the standard output. The term standard out abbreviated STDOUT is the regular console on the command line where results of command executions display. Linux bash shell regularly monitors this standard output location for any new output. Whenever the fresh output is found, the console prints it out to the console screen for users to see the output.

Standard Input

The STDIN read standard input is the default place on the bash shell where commands listen for input streams of data. As an example, when a user types a cd command without parameters, the stdin will look for input from the user, displaying what you punch in on your keyboard.

Redirection using Pipe

In bash, shell the Pipes are setup to connect output result from one command to another command as input. Piping is done by separating the two statements with the pipe symbol (|). Below is the illustration of this piping:

```
[ppeters@rad-srv ~]$echo "Linux is awesome for system administrators."
Linux is awesome for system administrators
[ppeters@rad-srv ~]$echo " Linux is awesome for system administrators " | sed "s/awesome/great/"

Linux is great for system administrators
```

A Basic Introduction to Search Tools

Linux administrators may need to know the location of a file or directory on the filesystem but may not know where to find it. Six bash commands can be used to search for it, including whatis, whereis, find, and locate, apropos, and which.

Introduction to Find

Below is the syntax of the **find** command:

[ppeters@rad-srv ~]$find search_path search_pattern

If the path for the file is not specified, the search when using find begins in the user's current working directory and searches down into all the subfolders.

The find command has many options that are reviewable through use of the find manual pages. The manual pages for the find command are found by entering **man find** at the bash terminal. The most utilized option is the **-name**, which directs our find command to look for files and directories with the specified string in their name.

[ppeters@rad-srv ~]$ find / -name file_name

The illustration of the find command above is a search for files in the root directory "/" with the name "file_name" string in their search pattern.

The Locate Command

The command locate s syntax is:

[ppeters@rad-srv ~]$locate search_pattern

The locate command enables us to see each file or folder that has the search_pattern string contained in the file or directory name. To locate a file or folder with the search pattern "finger," enter the following statement:

[ppeters@rad-srv ~]$locate pwd

The bash locate command makes use of the slocate data store to search for files and folders with the search pattern string "finger" in their names.

The locate command searches for strings patterns faster when the locate database is recent. That locate database is scheduled for auto-updates by running a cron task every night. In Linux, a cron job is a small utility that executes in the terminal background, executing a variety of scheduled responsibilities, for instance, making slocate database updates at 6 am every morning.

The updatedb command refreshes the slocate database on the command line interface.

Which, whatis and whereis Utilities

The which Command

Below is the syntax of the command:

[ppeters@rad-srv ~]$ which command_name

The above which statement returns the path of the binary, or executable, bash commands.

```
[ppeters@rad-srv ~]$which cd
/usr/bin/cd
[ppeters@rad-srv ~]$
```

The illustration of the which command above displays /usr/bin/cd.

The whereis Command

Below is the syntax of the whereis command:

```
[ppeters@rad-srv ~]$whereis command_name
```

The whereis command illustration below returns the paths of the find command, the binary file of the find command, the location of the source code, and the location of the find man page.

```
[ppeters@rad-srv~]$whereis find
/usr/bin/find                    /usr/share/man/man1p/find.1p.gz
/usr/share/man/man1/find.1.gz
[ppeters@rad-srv ~]$
```

The whatis Command

The syntax of the whatis command:

```
[ppeters@rad-srv ~]$ whatis command_name
```

The whatis command above displays details about the command_name from the command's man pages.

```
[ppeters@rad-srv ~]$whatis lp
```

Writing your First Shell Script

Your first bash scripting project is the Hello World example. Open your favorite editor and write a shell script file named as **examplebash.sh** containing the following lines.

Type in the shell terminal:

i.   **vi examplebash.sh**

ii. Press letter "I" on your keyboard to enter into insert mode

iii. Type the following in the **examplebash.sh**

```
#!/bin/bash
echo "This is my first example bash script" //display to the terminal screen
```

iv. After typing in the above then press **'ESC'** key on keyboard to leave insert mode and enter command mode

v.   After leaving insert mode, then type **':wq.'**

vi. The **:wq** command above writes the script and quits the Vi editor.

The initial line above is called the **shebang.** It informs the Linux shell that this is a bash script and that it should be executed on the **/bin/bash** shell. The ensuing line is just an *echo* statement, which displays the string of words passed to it to the terminal console.

29

After typing the Vi command to create the firstscript.sh, there's a need to give the shell script execute permissions to make it runnable. You can set the execute permission, as shown below:

```
[ppeters@rad-srv ~]$ chmod +x examplebash.sh
```

Executing the script has two options, as shown below. You can use either method to run the script after granting it execute permissions:

Option 1 using bash command
```
[ppeters@rad-srv ~]$ bash examplebash.sh
```

Option 2 using the ./ meta characters
```
[ppeters@rad-srv ~]$ ./examplebash.sh
```


Introduction to Scripting

A proper understanding of bash programming is essential for everyone who wants to be a Linux Engineer or administrator. It is important to remember that the bash programs are contained in the /etc /rc.d file. The programs are kept in this folder to ensure that Linux operating system runs them at startup and helps launch all the other Linux system services. To examine a program's reliability and possibly morph it, a deep comprehension of the startup scripts is extremely important.

It is not difficult to grasp the concept of bash programming, as bash scripting files can be developed in nibble-sized parts, and there are only a relatively small number of shell-specific operatives and training opportunities. The Linux bash scripting structure of programming is plain, even ostentatious, meaning it is close to the bash interface executing and gluing tools together, that only a few "laws regulate their usage." The majority of shell scripts that are small enough work during the initial phase, and checking and repairing errors even on longer bash scripts is simple.

A bash script is a quick and simple way to create a complex program model. Overseeing just a small subset of bash scripting activities is often a helpful beginning process in prototyping.

Shell programming goes way back to the traditional UNIX approach of separating a complex task into simpler subprograms and then grouping the components and utilities. Most Linux system users believe that bash scripting is a better way to help solve problems than to leveraging usage of one of the contemporary high-level languages, such as Java and Python, that attempt to have all features that suit everybody.

Conclusion

This chapter was a solid review of the basic Linux command line concepts covered in the first book in the Linux Command Line series. The reader was introduced to Linux operating system, Linux shell concepts, file search commands, file navigation, redirection basics, and finally showed how to write the first bash script. The next chapter is a review of the Linux file system, and a look at file system management and file system types before diving into disk management on the command line.

Chapter 2

File System Management

————————•◆•————————

This chapter is going to take the reader through the file system and filesystem management on the Linux command line. This chapter will detail what a file system and filesystem are before breaking down the types of filesystems we have in Linux and other non-Linux file systems that are inherently supported in Linux. The writer will also detail file permissions in Linux that apply to files and directories alike.

What is a File

Files are the central concept in the Linux filesystem. Files not only store information but also permit application programs to interconnect, provide access to hardware devices, represent folders of other files, act as pointers to information, or (virtually) connect machines over a network. Files are the principal notion behind the Linux operating system. In Linux, virtually everything is looked at as a file: regular or ordinary files, all folders, pipes to other processes, the interface to hardware devices, even pointers to files, also called links. Virtual files can also provide a user with access to kernel structures.

Though a file refers to a single entity, a file system describes the way files are stored on media. The term media includes the obvious hard disk drive, USB Disks, and CD-ROMs, as well as a network service or the RAM of your machine. Each file system type implements different properties. Not all file types can be stored on any file system, and not every file system type supports every medium. Files contain specific properties that define what type of file it is. Atypical property of all files is that they have a set of permissions, which is the designation that indicates which group it belongs to and who is the owner. Before we move onto file systems, ownership and permissions, we are going to take discuss the types of files we have in file systems.

- **Regular Files:** these store data on file systems. This is the ordinary type of file, a container for persistent data.

- **Directories:** Directories hold other files and other directories. Because modern file systems are organized in tree-like structures called hierarchies, you need something to hold the different levels of the hierarchy. That is a directory's purpose. If you're not used to referring to directories as files, remembering that they are nothing other than files containing a list of other files is important.

- **Special Device Files:** Special device files are merely virtual interfaces to a hardware device. There are mainly two types of device files, namely buffered and unbuffered hardware device files. Buffered files are named **block device** files, and the unbuffered files are called **character device** files.

- **Regular Pipes:** In Linux pipes are a communication link amongst two processes. The Linux operating system handles regular pipes like files inside the application. These pipes do not have a representation in Linux file systems. Pipes are noteworthy when you want to create an application program. At the user level, pipes are an easygoing technique to employ to join and concatenate commands and have the output from one command being the input to another command.

- **Named Pipes:** We have a different type of pipes that are similar to regular pipes, but the only difference is that they have a file system representation. Named pipes are also utilized for communication that occurs between processes. Named pipes can subsist exclusive of any access by processes.

- **Sockets:** In Linux, we have special files called sockets that are comparable to pipes and have similar purposes. The major distinction is that sockets are employed to work and connect over networks.

- **Hard Links:** In Linux, we have a type of file called a hard link, which is just a serial record in a file system directory. Hard links are essentially an association of a file name with an already existing file. They are merely an additional name for a file. In simple terms, we can refer to hard links as mirror copies of the actual file.

- **Soft Links:** Soft links, which are also called symbolic links, are a link or pointer to files in the file system.

Binaries or Executables aren't a distinct file type; that is why we have excluded them. In Linux systems, being executable or not is a property determined by the file permissions and does not depend on the type of file. Remember that certain files can be executed just by selected users or user groups.

Linux File System

We have been making use of the expression file system relatively routinely up to now exclusive of an operational meaning. The term, filesystem, has two distinctive meanings. File systems can be considered in the mold of Linux directory trees or Directory hierarchies in Linux. We term this the hierarchical structure of directories that comprise other directories and any kind of file. The second definition of the filesystem is that it is a specific type of data storage format such as ext3, ext4, btrfs, and so on, which shows that it is the lower-level format used on a given media to store files. Linux has support for more than 50 types of filesystems. Each of these filesystems employs unique metadata structures that define how the data is to be kept and accessed by users. The third and last meaning of a filesystem is a partition or logical volume that is formatted utilizing a particular filesystem and mounted on a defined mount point on the Linux directory tree hierarchy.

In Linux File systems organize files into logical hierarchical structures with directories, links. A file system organizes the block device data. This can be on a hard disk, a USB flash disk, RAM, or even a network connection to a remote system. The Linux file systems are not aware of the type of medium they are using. The device driver handles this. It's the job of the device driver to convert the address of a specific block to a physical location on a hard drive, a memory region.

The actual regular file system on a Linux system is the Extended two file system shortened to ext2. The first file system developed for Linux was the Minix file system termed Minixfs. Minixfs partitions were restricted to 64MB size, and filenames were limited to fourteen characters. The extended file system, introduced to the Linux world in April 1992, was mostly based on the Minixfs; it removed the previously mentioned limits, but still was far from perfect. This resulted in the creation of the ext2 file system. This development improved space allocation management to the ext file system, showed improved performance, approved the usage of unique flags in file administration, and made ext2 more extensible.

The VFS known fully as the Virtual File System appeared as a layer to the Linux OS when the ext file system was set up in the Linux kernel. The file system and the kernel were no longer a single module with this layer. A well-defined file system-kernel interface was established. Linux can allow a variety of different file systems via VFS. The kernel and the system programs are identical to all file systems. The VFS layer enables you to mount various file systems at the same time transparently.

The extended file system two is grounded on the supposition that the information is stored in equally sized blocks of memory on the storage device. Block sizes could well differ on distinct ext2 filesystems, and inside a single filesystem, totally, these chunks of memory are all of the same volume. The size is fixed when the utility mke2fs generates the Linux filesystem. The downside of this technique is that on the median, half the capacity of the block is lost for each document. If the size of the blocks is presumed to be1024 bytes, we will require two blocks for 1025 bytes file, just like a 2047 archive. Through managing data in this manner, you reduce the workload of the CPU.

In Linux, actual data may not be kept in blocks. Nearly all the blocks are expended to store data about the file system configuration. This extended file system called ext2 utilizes inode data structures for every file stored. An inode explains which blocks hold the data of the stipulated file, that is, its type, owner, and group, the permissions and the date of the last access, the last modification, and its creation date. In the Linux OS, inodes are kept in inode tables. In the same vein in Linux, a folder is merely a file that comprises of pointers or links to the inodes of the files inside this folder.

Purpose of filesystems

In Linux, like in any other operating system, the most crucial requirement is hard disk space, which carries data and information. In operating systems, a filesystem was developed to supply a place where data is stored. However, we have several file system functions that are born of the requirement.

Every Unix-like operating system needs to specify a system namespace, which is the naming and administrative methodology. This namespace is required to explain what a file could be named independent of the full group of availed characters, incorporating the length of a file and the group of characters that could be used for filenames. It also describes the logical structure of the information on a drive, such as the use of folders to arrange documents rather than putting them all together in a large, massive folder combination of files.

Only after the filesystem namespace is specified, a system of metadata is needed to include the logical basis for that filesystem namespace. It comprises the system data structures required to sustain a hierarchical folder structure; frameworks to specify what sections of disk space will be used and which are available; frameworks to enable file or folder titles to be maintained; details on files such as their size and periods they are generated, changed or last accessed; and position and layout of the document. Certain metadata, such as logical volumes and partitions, are used to store foremost information concerning disk sectors. This foremost metadata and the configurations it represents comprise the data defining the filesystem saved on the drive or partition but is detached from and sovereign of the filesystem metadata.

Filesystems often include an Application Programming Interface (API), which provides access to process function calls that control filesystem artifacts such as files and folders. APIs set up functions such as creating, transferring, and deleting files. It also offers algorithms that decide items like where a document is located on a file system. These algorithms can compensate for objectives such as speed or mitigate disk fragmentation.

The Linux security model helps to ensure that users are allowed only their own files and not those of other users or the operating system itself. The system also includes a security model, which is a framework for determining access rights to files and directories.

The ultimate building block is the software required to implement all of these functions. Linux uses a two-part software implementation as a way to improve both system and programmer efficiency.

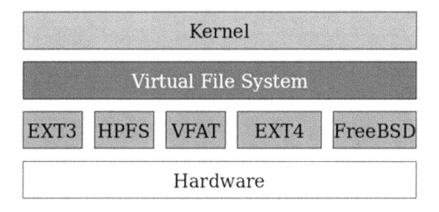

Linux OS's virtual filesystem is the first component of this two-part architecture. The virtual filesystem presents one set of instructions to access all forms of file systems for the kernel and developers. The code for the virtual filesystem calls a device driver for communication with different filesystem forms. The final part of the architecture is the filesystem-specific application device drivers. The application driver perceives the default collection of filesystem commands to those unique to the partition type and logical volume class of filesystems.

File System Types

The section above showed that we have a **Linux file system** and **Linux filesystem**. In this section of the book, we are going to detail some Linux filesystems such as ext, ext2, ext3, Reiserfs, and other filesystems that Linux supports, such as MS-DOS, uMS-DOS, vfat, proc, NFS, iso9660, hpfs, sysv, smb, ncpfs.

Much of the detail about the file system types in Linux can be read from manual pages through the usage of the man command. To get more information about the file systems that are available in Linux, we use the command man fs.

Manual page listing of file systems

Minix a filesystem operated, which was operating in the Minix OS. This was the first filesystem developed for Linux. This fs had a selection of flaws; for instance, it has restriction on the partition size to 64MB, and it also has short filenames, a single time stamp.

ext This fs is commonly named the extended file system. This filesystem was an improvement on the Minix filesystem. This extended filesystem has entirely been replaced by a second variety of the extended filesystem called the ext2 in short. Ext has been removed from the Linux kernel.

ext2 This filesystem is loaded. It is used in the Linux OS equally for static disk drives and removable disk drives. This subsequent extended **ext2** was created to serve as a substitute to the **ext** filesystem. This ext2 filesystem offers excellent value in relation to CPU usage and effectiveness.

ext3 This filesystem is the third extended filesystem that has journaling added to it. The third extended fs is an improvement to the ext2 fs. It is easy to toggle back and forth between these two filesystems ext2 and ext3.

Reiserfs This filesystem was developed by Hans Reiser for integration into the 2.4.1 kernel

XFS Called the Extents File System. This is a high octane 64-bit journaling filesystem, created in 1993 by silicon graphics also known as SGI. Supports sizes of about eight exbibytes

JFS This is a filesystem that journals or keeps track of changes not yet dedicated to the file system's core part

xiafs **This is a file system that** was created and meant for stability, safety through extension of the Minix filesystem code.   This filesystem delivers the essential demanded qualities exclusive of unwarranted difficulty.   The **xia** filesystem was discontinued and is no longer on the Linux kernel.

Vfat This is an extended DOS fs which was utilized for Microsoft Windows95 and Windows NT. VFAT added the ability that permitted usage of extended filenames in the MSDOS filesystem.

proc this is a quasi-filesystem utilized as a boundary to the Linux kernel record configurations instead of reading and deducing information from /dev/kmem file.

The Linux filesystem is built on Linux disk partition using the *mkfs* command. Nonetheless, if you are preparing to format the entire hard disk drive, exploiting the *fdisk* utility is very simple. After using fdisk to partition your filesystem, it is important to remember that the filesystem has to be mounted beforehand so that you can do anything on it.

Disk Partitioning Schemes

The File System arrangement is a hierarchical tree of folders and subfolders. In Linux, as in any other operating system, the physical assets with the data are **mounted** at particular places on the file system named **mount points**. The root of the hierarchical tree structure is titled the **root** directory and is represented by a forward slash "/." When the computer boots, the boot loader dictates the device to mount at the root. The "leaves" on any tree structure are called subdirectories. While installation is ongoing, the hard drive is partitioned and a size and a mount point for each partition assigned.

On functioning Linux systems, all attached hard disks are denoted by entries in the **/dev** directory. The Linux kernel interconnects with devices using a distinctive major/minor duo grouping. All major digits are found the directory **/proc/devices**. For instance, the initial IDE controller's major number is **3**: 1 – ramdisk, 2 – fd, and 3- ide0 . Hard disk descriptors in **/dev** begin with *hd* (IDE) or *sd* (SCSI. Since a Linux system can have more than one block device, an additional letter is added to the descriptor to indicate which device is being considered.

Physical block	devices
HAD	Primary Master
HDB	Primary Slave
HDC	Secondary Master
HDD	Secondary Slave
SDA	First SCSI disk
SDB	Second SCSI disk

In Linux, Disks can additionally be subdivided. To maintain a record of the partitions, a number is appended at the end of each physical device name to show the subdivisions.

Numbered	Partitions
hda1	partition one on hard disk drive number 1
hda2	Partition 2 on the hard disk drive number 1
sdc3	Partition 3 on SCSI disk drive number 3

IDE disk types permit only four *primary* partitions, one of which can be *extended*. The extended partition can further be divided into *logical* partitions. There can be a maximum of 64 partitions on an IDE disk and 16 on a SCSI disk. The primary partitions (1,2,3,4) and (1,2,5,6,7,8).

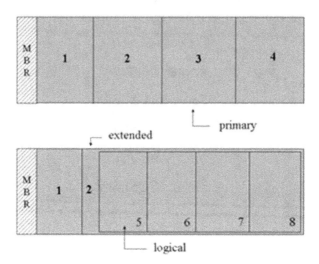

During the Linux installation stage, the administrator is required to make numerous partitions to keep the Linux file system. A typical Linux system will need two or more disk partitions:

- **The root partition:** This is the partition where / (the root directory) will be located on a Linux system. It is important not to confuse this partition with the /root directory, which is the home directory of the superuser.

- **A swap partition:** This is the hard disk space on your machine that can be used as virtual memory. Virtual memory allows your computer to run large programs and perform complex tasks even if it does not have enough physical RAM to do the job.

Devices Management

Introduction

In this section of the book, the reader is going to learn about designing and making Linux file system partitions and file systems, file permissions, monitoring disk usage, and file system mounting and unmounting. We need to define a partition before we dive into the partitioning phase. A hard disk partition is defined as storage space on a hard drive. Disk partitioning is the act or practice of dividing the hard disk storage space into separate data areas known as partitions.

Creating Linux Partitions

One has the choice to associate a piece of hardware to a Linux folder or directory. For example, the root directory "/" which is more or less like the C:\ drive for Windows OS might be mapped to the **/dev/sda2** partition, and the subdirectory **/boot** could correspond to the partition **/dev/sda3**. The Linux partition **/dev/sda3** is said to be **mounted** on the **/boot** directory". The Filesystem folder directory on which a storage or block device is attached to is called a file system **mount point**.

While installing the operating system, Linux administrators are presented with the choice of creating new partitions and associating each partition to a mount point. For advanced users this is done in two steps in the Linux command line:

- Utilizing the **fdisk** utility to produce the new disk partitions

- Associate a mount point with each of the disk partitions

For intermediate users, most Linux variants include a user-friendly tool that does both these steps. RedHat proved incredibly successful over projects like Debian and that was down to the introduction of intuitive installation tools such as **DiskDruid**. Finally the newest distributions are ideal for both the busy sysadmin and beginners because they will automatically assign a partition scheme.

Once the OS has been installed,fdisk can be used to configure new partitions. Net, we turn our attention to the fdisk syntax.

1) Start partitioning the first hard drive:

```
[ppeters@rad-srv ~]$      fdisk /dev/hda
```

2) You will be presented with the screen output below

```
[root@rad-srv ~]# fdisk /dev/hda

The number of cylinders for this disk is set to 9729.
There is nothing wrong with that, but this is larger than 1024,
and could in certain setups cause problems with:
1) software that runs at boot time (e.g., old versions of LILO)
2) booting and partitioning software from other OSs
   (e.g., DOS FDISK, OS/2 FDISK)

Command (m for help):
```

3) Type **m** for help.

```
Command (m for help): m
Command action
```

```
a   toggle a bootable flag
b   edit bsd disklabel
c   toggle the dos compatibility flag
d   delete a partition
l   list known partition types
m   print this menu
n   add a new partition
o   create a new empty DOS partition table
p   print the partition table
q   quit without saving changes
s   create a new empty Sun disklabel
t   change a partition's system-id
u   change display/entry units
v   verify the partition table
w   write table to disk and exit
x   extra functionality (experts only)

Command (m for help):
```

4) Type **n** to create a new partition. Below is the prompt you get

```
Command (m for help): n
Command action
   e   extended
   p   primary partition (1-4)
```

After selecting either e or p and selecting partition number, you move to the next phase.

5) To write the changes to disk type **w**.

6) REBOOT.

These six points outline the steps you would follow to create new partitions. The last point is often overlooked. This forces the partition table in the master boot record **MBR** to be reread.

NOTICE

You need to create a filesystem on a new partition with **mkfs** or **mke2fs** before using it

---

Managing Block Devices in Linux
At Linux boot time, the Linux file **/etc/fstab** assigns mount points for all block devices in the filesystem.

The organization of the /etc/fstab file is shown below:

device mount-point fstype options dump-number fsck-number

Illustration of the /etc/fstab file

```
[root@rad-srv ~]# cat /etc/fstab
/dev/VolGroup00/LogVol00 /          ext3   defaults      1 1
LABEL=/boot          /boot          ext3   defaults      1 2
tmpfs                /dev/shm       tmpfs  defaults      0 0
devpts               /dev/pts       devpts gid=5,mode=620 0 0
sysfs                /sys           sysfs  defaults      0 0
proc                 /proc          defaults      0 0
/dev/VolGroup00/LogVol01 swap          defaults      0 0
[root@rad-srv ~]#
```

On a running system the **/etc/fstab** file also acts as a *shortcut* for assigning a resource to a specific directory.

The **mount** utility reads **fstab** and gathers details about where to mount the resource. Notice that some of the devices are accessed using a label. Labels are assigned to devices with the **tune2fs** tool:

```
[root@rad-srv ~]# tune2fs -L /usr/local /dev/hdb12
```

Mount point options

rw, ro   Mount point read and write the read-only options

Users   All users can read and unmount the device

user   The user can unmount the device

owner   the device will change its permission and belong to the user that mounted it

usrquota   start user quotas on the device

grpquota   start group quotas on the device

Nugget

Learn that command **mount -a** with option **-a** mounts all noauto filesystems into the **/etc/fstab** that are unmounted

Logical Volume Management

In Linux, we have a technique called Logical volume management, which is widely abbreviated as LVM. LVM is a method of virtualization of Linux disk storage that provides Linux system administrators with a more adaptable method than conventional disk partitioning methods used for managing disk storage capacity. This form of disk management mechanism originates in the

Linux operating system's device driver block. This functions by separating storage of physical volumes, also known by their short name PVs into physical extents abbreviated PEs. The PEs are them linked to logical extents known by their short name LEs that are subsequently combined into a group of storage volumes abbreviated as VGs. The volume groups are associated with logical volumes shortened to LVs, which function as simulated or virtual hard disk file system partitions and can be controlled by using LVM as such.

LVM's main objective is to simplify the management of numerous end-users ' often overlapping storage requirements. The Linux system administrator does not need to reserve all hard disk storage capacity at the beginning setup process utilizing the volume management technique. Some may be retained for future distribution in inventory. The Linux system administrator uses LVM to theoretically fragment serial data or merge partitions to improve throughput and make it simpler to resize and subsequently transfer the volumes of space as desired. With different user classes within the organization, data volumes may be specified, and additional capacity can be introduced to a given group as required without allowing relocation of client files to allow the most effective use of space. Once old drives are replaced, the data contained in them can be converted into new drives— preferably without interrupting service availability for system's end users.

Logical volume management is a popular procedure for implementing logical or virtual alternately physical storage. With this LVM technique, disk logical or virtual compartments can span through numerous physical drives that can incidentally be resized while they are working. To start with LVM, we divide the physical disk into one or more physical extents or volumes, and then afterward, we create logical volume groups by combining the PVs. The disk volume groups or VGs are a combination of PVs from many physical hard disks.

LVM Advantages

Logical volume management technique provides the Linux user with many advantages. LVM makes managing partitions a lot easier. Most Linux filesystems may be expanded and expanding a partition (or Logical Volume as they're called in LVM) is a LOT easier than it is with MBR or GPT partition tables. The main reason it is use is because of the enhanced flexibility it provides.

When you create the setup, it is important that all the disks are not allocated to your Logical Volumes, leave some slack. When the filesystems expand to where they require more space, Expand it using some of your saved space. This is a straightforward operation, and unlike MBR/GPT, the actual data area doesn't even have to be contiguous.

LVM extends the code-path that takes data to actual drives, but it is very battle-tested by now.

The major advantage is that LVM affords the system administrator more flexibility and helps in abstracting the physical disks. The next advantage is that the storage's Logical volumes can be rescaled while they are online and mounted and are reachable by the data store or file system, eliminating the stoppage related to adding or deleting storage from a Linux server. We do not need to restart a machine when dealing with Logical volumes. Information from a possibly defective or impaired physical disk device might be transferred to an alternative disk storage device that is latest, speedier, or extra resistant, while the primary logical volume continues running online and reachable. Also, we can build logical volumes by grouping numerous physical hard disk devices to increase performance through a technique called disk striping or improved disk redundancy through the methods of disk mirroring and I/O multipathing. In Linux Logical disk volume snapshots can be generated to represent the precise state of the logical volume at a particular point-in-time, permitting accurate backups to continue concurrently with routine system functioning.

LVM Architecture

All Linux system users must have a fundamental comprehension of how storage devices are organized in Logical Volume Management.

LVM Storage Management Structures

LVM operates by putting layers of abstraction atop storage physical devices. LVM uses three primary and elementary layers, starting with the most original, are named Physical Volumes, Volume Groups, and Logical Volumes.

LVM Physical Volumes

The LVM tool uses the prefix pv for all actions and operations to be carried out on Physical volumes. **All** physical storage devices or further disk-like devices, for instance, those devices produced by the kernel's device-mapper, such as RAID arrays, are employed by the Logical Volume Manager as the basic building blocks for advanced levels of abstraction. In LVM Physical volumes are just ordinary storage devices. LVM writes a header to the device to allocate it for management.

LVM Volume Groups

The LVM facility uses the vg prefix for everything that pertains to volume groups. All commands that are associated with volume groups start with the prefix vg. LVM chains together some physical disk volumes into a single pool of storage identified as the LVM volume groups. Volume groups in LVM hide away the features of the primary disk devices and work as a combined single logical device with pooled storage capacity of the constituent physical volumes.

Logical Volumes

The LVM function utilizes the word lv as the prefix for commands and actions that have a bearing on the Logical volume. The lv prefix is prepended to commands that are used in the creation and management of Logical volumes. LVM takes the volume groups created from the Physical volumes and breaks them up into slices, which are called the logical volumes. These Logical volumes are operationally alike to file system partitions on a hard disk; however, they have more elasticity. Logical volumes are the principal constituent that all users and applications will cooperate with.

Steps to Setup LVM

The first step is for the Administrator to login into the system with their user ID; the second stage is to check the disks that are available to be worked on by the LVM utility. The initial step to creating physical volumes is to mark the physical devices through the usage of **lvmdiskscan.**

Marking Physical Volumes

```
ppeters@rad-srv:~$ sudo lvmdiskscan
[sudo] password for ppeters:
 /dev/sda1 [    <16.00 GiB]
 /dev/sda5 [    <4.00 GiB]
 /dev/sdb [    20.00 GiB]
 1 disk
 2 partitions
 0 LVM physical volume whole disks
 0 LVM physical volumes
ppeters@rad-srv:~$
```

Alternatively you could use fdisk

```
ppeters@rad-srv:~$ sudo fdisk -l
Disk /dev/sda: 20 GiB, 21474836480 bytes, 41943040 sectors
Disk model: VMware Virtual S
Units: sectors of 1 * 512 = 512 bytes
Sector size (logical/physical): 512 bytes / 512 bytes
I/O size (minimum/optimal): 512 bytes / 512 bytes
Disklabel type: dos
Disk identifier: 0x6ee4ff5e
Device    Boot    Start    End  Sectors Size Id Type
```

/dev/sda1 *   2048 33554431 33552384 16G 83 Linux

/dev/sda2   33556478 41940991 8384514   4G 5 Extended

/dev/sda5   33556480 41940991 8384512   4G 82 Linux

swap / Solaris

Disk /dev/sdb: 20 GiB, 21474836480 bytes, 41943040 sectors

Disk model: VMware Virtual S

Units: sectors of 1 * 512 = 512 bytes

Sector size (logical/physical): 512 bytes / 512 bytes

I/O size (minimum/optimal): 512 bytes / 512 bytes

ppeters@rad-srv:~$

Creating and Displaying the Created PV

ppeters@rad-srv:~$ sudo pvcreate /dev/sdb

 Physical volume "/dev/sdb" successfully created.

ppeters@rad-srv:~$ sudo pvdisplay

 "/dev/sdb" is a new physical volume of "20.00 GiB"

 --- NEW Physical volume ---

 PV Name   /dev/sdb

 VG Name

 PV Size   20.00 GiB

 Allocatable   NO

 PE Size   0

 Total PE   0

 Free PE   0

 Allocated PE   0

PV UUID	UjFu4U-xJEf-VOZW-TqLu-jw9q-UyOX-m4UUFx

The command above was written to create a physical volume on /dev/sdb and the second command pvdisplay was executed to show the Physical volume created above

Creating the VG (Volume Group)

The command vgcreate rad-srv-vg /dev/sdb was used to create the volume group and also executed the vgdisplay command to display the created volume group, as shown below.

```
ppeters@rad-srv:~$ sudo vgcreate rad-srv-vg /dev/sdb
  Volume group "rad-srv-vg" successfully created
ppeters@rad-srv:~$ sudo vgdisplay
  --- Volume group ---
  VG Name              rad-srv-vg
  System ID
  Format          lvm2
  Metadata Areas     1
  Metadata Sequence No  1
  VG Access          read/write
  VG Status          resizable
  MAX LV            0
  Cur LV            0
  Open LV           0
  Max PV            0
  Cur PV            1
  Act PV            1
```

```
VG Size          <20.00 GiB
PE Size          4.00 MiB
Total PE         5119
Alloc PE / Size    0 / 0
Free  PE / Size   5119 / <20.00 GiB
VG UUID            02s5Jx-01I6-qCQR-FrA5-oDWV-nWdO-
j6PtOw


ppeters@rad-srv:~$
```

Running the lvmdiskscan, we can see that we have an LVM managed storage disk, as shown below.

```
ppeters@rad-srv:~$ sudo lvmdiskscan
/dev/sda1 [    <16.00 GiB]
/dev/sda5 [    <4.00 GiB]
/dev/sdb  [    20.00 GiB] LVM physical volume
0 disks
2 partitions
1 LVM physical volume whole disk
0 LVM physical volumes
ppeters@rad-srv:~$
```

After confirming that we have our Physical volume and Volume group, we can go ahead and create the virtual partition of the volume group using the lvcreate command as detailed in the next section.

Creating the Logical Volume (LV)

We are creating a 2GB logical volume below using the command lvcreate –L2048 –n rad-srv-lv01 rad-srv-vg, as shown by the illustration below. The second line of the command is an lvdisplay command to show the newly created Logical Volume.

```
ppeters@rad-srv:~$ sudo lvcreate -L2048 -n rad-srv-lv01 rad-
srv-vg
  Logical volume "rad-srv-lv01" created.
ppeters@rad-srv:~$ sudo lvdisplay
  --- Logical volume ---
  LV Path            /dev/rad-srv-vg/rad-srv-lv01
  LV Name            rad-srv-lv01
  VG Name            rad-srv-vg
  LV UUID            3iVSKv-HtEb-gaWb-OEAN-wk9N-JpyR-
zGRMkb
  LV Write Access    read/write
  LV Creation host, time rad-srv, 2019-11-18 15:31:50 +0200
  LV Status          available
  # open             0
  LV Size            2.00 GiB
  Current LE         512
  Segments           1
  Allocation         inherit
  Read ahead sectors auto
  - currently set to  256
  Block device       254:0
```

ppeters@rad-srv:~$

In LVM, we can create stripped logical volumes as shown by the illustration below:

```
ppeters@rad-srv:~$ sudo lvcreate -i1 -I4 --size 5G -n stripped-lv rad-srv-vg
  Ignoring stripesize argument with single stripe.
  Logical volume "stripped-lv" created.
ppeters@rad-srv:~$ sudo lvdisplay
  --- Logical volume ---
  LV Path                /dev/rad-srv-vg/rad-srv-lv01
  LV Name                rad-srv-lv01
  VG Name                rad-srv-vg
  LV UUID                3iVSKv-HtEb-gaWb-OEAN-wk9N-JpyR-zGRMkb
  LV Write Access        read/write
  LV Creation host, time rad-srv, 2019-11-18 15:31:50 +0200
  LV Status              available
  # open                 0
  LV Size                2.00 GiB
  Current LE             512
  Segments               1
  Allocation             inherit
  Read ahead sectors     auto
  - currently set to     256
  Block device           254:0

  --- Logical volume ---
```

```
LV Path              /dev/rad-srv-vg/stripped-lv
LV Name              stripped-lv
VG Name              rad-srv-vg
LV UUID                    XRv8er-NJ4N-yYea-0AqV-Zh5z-rEha-
Z0Sstd
LV Write Access      read/write
LV Creation host, time rad-srv, 2019-11-18 15:36:16 +0200
LV Status            available
# open               0
LV Size              5.00 GiB
Current LE           1280
Segments             1
Allocation           inherit
Read ahead sectors    auto
- currently set to    256
Block device          254:1

ppeters@rad-srv:~$
```

After the creation of the Logical volumes and confirming that it has been created using the lvdisplay command, we can then make a file system on the logical volume. We use the mkfs tool and then specify the type of the file system that we want on the logical volume or virtual partition.

```
mkfs –t ext4 /dev/rad-srv-vg/rad-srv-lv01
ppeters@rad-srv:~$ sudo mkfs -t ext4 /dev/rad-srv-vg/rad-srv-lv01
lv01
mke2fs 1.44.5 (15-Dec-2018)
```

```
Creating filesystem with 524288 4k blocks and 131072 inodes
Filesystem UUID: e72a149f-2e24-4c55-9c8f-4e656c615828
Superblock backups stored on blocks:
    32768, 98304, 163840, 229376, 294912

Allocating group tables: done
Writing inode tables: done
Creating journal (16384 blocks): done
Writing superblocks and filesystem accounting information:
done
```

After making the file system, the next step is to create a directory using the mkdir command. This directory will be used as the mount point for the logical volume called rad-srv-lv01 we created above.

```
ppeters@rad-srv:~$ sudo mkdir /lvm_directory
ppeters@rad-srv:~$ sudo mount /dev/rad-srv-vg/rad-srv-lv01
/lvm_directory/
ppeters@rad-srv:~$
```

After creating the filesystem and the lvm_directory folder, we then mount our logical volume on that directory so that our users can use it. We can do df -h command to verify if the rad-srv-lv01 is mounted on the newly created lvm_directory as illustrated below

```
ppeters@rad-srv:~$ df -h
Filesystem              Size  Used Avail Use% Mounted on
udev                    2.0G     0 2.0G   0% /dev
tmpfs                   393M   11M 382M   3% /run
/dev/sda1                16G  1.1G  14G   8% /
```

```
tmpfs                    2.0G   0 2.0G  0% /dev/shm
tmpfs                    5.0M   0 5.0M  0% /run/lock
tmpfs                    2.0G   0 2.0G  0% /sys/fs/cgroup
tmpfs                    393M   0 393M  0% /run/user/1000
/dev/mapper/rad--srv--vg-rad--srv--lv01 2.0G 6.0M 1.8G 1%
/lvm_directory
ppeters@rad-srv:~$
```

After mount, it is important to make an entry in **/etc/fstab** file if we desire for the logical volume to be permanently mounted.

Reducing Logical Volume size?

We are planning to reduce the size of the logical volume "rad-srv-lv01" logical volume.

Step 1: we need to execute the unmount command to unmount from /lvm_directory as shown below and verify using df -h that the mount has been removed.

```
ppeters@rad-srv:~$ sudo umount /dev/mapper/rad--srv--vg-rad--srv--lv01
ppeters@rad-srv:~$ df -h
Filesystem    Size  Used Avail Use% Mounted on
udev          2.0G   0 2.0G  0% /dev
tmpfs         393M  11M 382M  3% /run
/dev/sda1      16G 1.1G  14G  8% /
tmpfs         2.0G   0 2.0G  0% /dev/shm
tmpfs         5.0M   0 5.0M  0% /run/lock
tmpfs         2.0G   0 2.0G  0% /sys/fs/cgroup
tmpfs         393M   0 393M  0% /run/user/1000
ppeters@rad-srv:~$
```

Step 2: The next step is to perform a filesystem check e2fsck -f /dev/mapper/rad—srv—vg-rad—srv—lv01

ppeters@rad-srv:~$ sudo e2fsck -f /dev/mapper/rad--srv--vg-rad--srv--lv01

e2fsck 1.44.5 (15-Dec-2018)

Pass 1: Checking inodes, blocks, and sizes

Pass 2: Checking directory structure

Pass 3: Checking directory connectivity

Pass 4: Checking reference counts

Pass 5: Checking group summary information

/dev/mapper/rad--srv--vg-rad--srv--lv01: 11/131072 files (0.0% non-contiguous), 26156/524288 blocks

ppeters@rad-srv:~$

Step 3: We can then resize the Logical volume using the following command resize2fs to 1G

ppeters@rad-srv:~$ sudo resize2fs /dev/mapper/rad--srv--vg-rad--srv--lv01 1G

resize2fs 1.44.5 (15-Dec-2018)

Resizing the filesystem on /dev/mapper/rad--srv--vg-rad--srv--lv01 to 262144 (4k) blocks.

The filesystem on /dev/mapper/rad--srv--vg-rad--srv--lv01 is now 262144 (4k) blocks long.

ppeters@rad-srv:~$

Step 4: We can lvreduce -L 8G /dev/mapper/rad—srv—vg-rad—
srv—lv01

```
ppeters@rad-srv:~$ sudo lvreduce -L 1G /dev/mapper/rad--srv--vg-
rad--srv--lv01
  WARNING: Reducing active logical volume to 1.00 GiB.
  THIS MAY DESTROY YOUR DATA (filesystem etc.)
Do you really want to reduce rad-srv-vg/rad-srv-lv01? [y/n]: y
  Size of logical volume rad-srv-vg/rad-srv-lv01 changed from 2.00
GiB (512 extents) to 1.00 GiB (256 extents).
  Logical volume rad-srv-vg/rad-srv-lv01 successfully resized.
ppeters@rad-srv:~$
```

Logical volume validation

We can use the Logical volume command to display the reduced
Logical Volume.

```
ppeters@rad-srv:~$ sudo lvs
  LV          VG         Attr      LSize Pool Origin Data% Meta% Move
Log Cpy%Sync Convert
  rad-srv-lv01 rad-srv-vg -wi-a----- 1.00g
  stripped-lv  rad-srv-vg -wi-a----- 5.00g
ppeters@rad-srv:~$
```

Increasing LV Online

Step 1: Use the **vgs** command to check the amount of available
space on the volume group.

Check either space available or not in VG using following
command # vgs or vgdisplay. If enough space available then go
ahead and execute the below commands

64

```
ppeters@rad-srv:~$ sudo vgs
 VG        #PV #LV #SN Attr   VSize   VFree
 rad-srv-vg  1  2  0 wz--n- <20.00g <14.00g
ppeters@rad-srv:~$
```

Step 2: We can extend the logical volume using lvextend

```
ppeters@rad-srv:~$ sudo lvextend -L +4000M /dev/mapper/rad--srv--
vg-rad--srv--lv01
 Size of logical volume rad-srv-vg/rad-srv-lv01 changed from 1.00
GiB (256 extents) to <4.91 GiB (1256 extents).
 Logical volume rad-srv-vg/rad-srv-lv01 successfully resized.
ppeters@rad-srv:~$
```

Step 3: After extending we can then resize the Logical volume
using the following command; resize2fs /dev/mapper/ rad--
srv--vg-rad--srv--lv01

```
ppeters@rad-srv:~$ sudo resize2fs /dev/mapper/rad--srv--vg-rad--srv-
-lv01
resize2fs 1.44.5 (15-Dec-2018)
Resizing the filesystem on /dev/mapper/rad--srv--vg-rad--srv--lv01 to
1286144 (4k) blocks.
The filesystem on /dev/mapper/rad--srv--vg-rad--srv--lv01 is now
1286144 (4k) blocks long.

ppeters@rad-srv:~$
```

Step 4:

```
ppeters@rad-srv:~$ sudo e2fsck -f /dev/mapper/rad--srv--vg-rad--srv-
-lv01
e2fsck 1.44.5 (15-Dec-2018)
```

```
Pass 1: Checking inodes, blocks, and sizes
Pass 2: Checking directory structure
Pass 3: Checking directory connectivity
Pass 4: Checking reference counts
Pass 5: Checking group summary information
/dev/mapper/rad--srv--vg-rad--srv--lv01: 11/327680 files (0.0% non-
contiguous), 39006/1286144 blocks
ppeters@rad-srv:~$
```

Removing an LV

Step 1: The first step is to unmount the logical volume using the umount /lvm_directory command

Step 2: Delete the logical volume entry in /etc/fstab file

Step 3: After clearing the /etc/fstab file you then use the **lvremove** command to remove the logical volume using its path /dev/rad-srv-vg/rad-srv-lv01

Creating Snapshots in LVM

Step 1: Create the snapshot using the lvcreate command with -s option for snapshots

Step 2: Create directory snapshots_dir for use with the snapshots logical volume

Step 3: The last step is to mount the logical volume snap image on /snapshots_dir

```
ppeters@rad-srv:~$ sudo lvcreate -L1024M -s -n rad-srv-snapshot
/dev/rad-srv-vg/rad-srv-lv01
  Logical volume "rad-srv-snapshot" created.
```

66

```
ppeters@rad-srv:~$ mkdir /snapshots_dir
mkdir: cannot create directory '/snapshots_dir': Permission denied
ppeters@rad-srv:~$ sudo mkdir /snapshots_dir
ppeters@rad-srv:~$ mount /dev/rad-srv-vg/rad-srv-
rad-srv-lv01    rad-srv-snapshot
ppeters@rad-srv:~$ sudo  mount  /dev/rad-srv-vg/rad-srv-snapshot
/snapshots_dir/
ppeters@rad-srv:~$ df -h
Filesystem                Size  Used Avail Use% Mounted on
udev                      2.0G   0 2.0G  0% /dev
tmpfs                     393M  11M 382M  3% /run
/dev/sda1                 16G 1.1G  14G  8% /
tmpfs                     2.0G   0 2.0G  0% /dev/shm
tmpfs                     5.0M   0 5.0M  0% /run/lock
tmpfs                     2.0G   0 2.0G  0% /sys/fs/cgroup
tmpfs                     393M   0 393M  0% /run/user/1000
/dev/mapper/rad--srv--vg-rad--srv--snapshot 4.8G 8.0M 4.5G  1%
/snapshots_dir
ppeters@rad-srv:~$
```

Chapter 3

File & Directory Permissions

————•◆•————

The Linux operating system takes care of the file system and directory access through the usage of the file system permissions block. The file permission block is an integral segment of Linux's inode table records for every file and Linux directory. The Linux user can show the file and directory permissions by using the long directory listing command **ls -l** for regular files and **ls -ld** for all folders.

When we use the **ls -l** and **ls -ld** commands, the output shows the file permissions column as the first section of the output result. The permissions block for long listing of folders and files is built up of ten characters. Every file or folder on a Linux filesystem, irrespective of its type or kind, is organized by the Linux file system's permission block. The file system's permissions block consists of two distinctive types of data. The very first symbol or character in the permissions block is a sign of file type, and the next nine characters are access level permissions. This subsequent book section discusses these two types of information.

Linux File Types

In the file and folder permissions column, our operating system employs the first character or symbol to display the type of file inputted in the Linux inode table. Since Linux does not distinguish between files and folders in the inode table, this character is the only way for the operating system to understand whether the entry corresponds to a standard folder or directory. In Linux folders are not tangible entities on the Linux filesystem; nevertheless, directories are merely used to organizing the files and subsequent subdirectories in the filesystem. The records for files and folders in the inode data structure are very equivalent.

The Linux operating system supports numerous useful file types, which are represented by a distinct symbol or character value. These symbols or characters are appended as the first symbol in the file permissions column of the long listing. Below we have the very communal file type letterings that are used in the Linux operating system:

-	Regular and ordinary file
b	This character represents buffered or block devices
c	This character represents unbuffered or character devices
d	This character represents a folder known in Linux as a directory
l	This character or letter represents a link

Some variants of Linux support a set of unique file types regarded as special types such as **s,** which stands for special file; however, these file types are infrequently used.

In the Linux system, we have regular and ordinary files. The ordinary or regular file can be documents, a program or application, a text file, or any file that has data whether openly accessible by the user or not. The dash character signifies these common files "–"

also called the hyphen in the Linux file type section of the permissions block. Ordinary and regular files are all the files created by users of the Linux system. Permissions can be set, modified, and configured in Linux using the **chmod utility**. In Linux, we have three classifications of ownership for files and directories alike. Below we have the following symbolic or character values for the file system **ownership** fields:

u: this character represents a user as recorded in the **/etc/passwd file**

g: this character represents a user group with an entry in the file **/etc/group**

o: this letter represents everyone else otherwise referred to as **other.**

Illustration of File Permissions

```
[root@rad-srv /]# ls -l jamboard-backup.tar.gz
-rw-r--r-- 1 root 212992 Oct  1  2019 jamboard-backup.tar.gz
[root@rad-srv /]#
```

Changing Permissions

```
[root@rad-srv /]# chmod g=r,o-r jamboard-backup.tar.gz
[root@rad-srv /]# ls -l jamboard-backup.tar.gz
-rw-r----- 1 root 212992 Oct  1  2019 jamboard-backup.tar.gz
[root@rad-srv /]#
```

Example 2: Using chmod to Change Permissions

```
[root@rad-srv /]# chmod g+w commerce-backup.tar.gz
```

```
[root@rad-srv /]# ls -l commerce-backup.tar.gz
-rw-rw---- 1 root 212992 Oct 1 2019 commerce-backup.tar.gz
[root@rad-srv /]#
```

Changing User and Group

```
[root@rad-srv /]# chown ppeterszw commerce-backup.tar.gz
[root@rad-srv /]# ls -l commerce-backup.tar.gz
-rw-rw---- 1 ppeterszw root 212992 Oct 1 2012 commerce-
backup.tar.gz
[root@rad-srv /]#
```

Changing Group Example

```
[root@rad-srv /]# chgrp ppeterszw commerce-backup.tar.gz
[root@rad-srv /]# ls -l commerce-backup.tar.gz
-rw-rw---- 1 ppeterszw 212992 Oct 1 2012 commerce-
backup.tar.gz
[root@rad-srv /]#
```

NUGGET

A useful option for **chmod**, **chown,** and **chgrp** is the **–R,** which recursively changes ownership and permissions through all files and directories indicated.

Symbolic and Octal Notation

Linux file permissions are **read** represented by letter **r**, write represented by symbol **w,** and execute permission represented by **x**. The table below shows the octal values of these permissions.

Octal and Symbolic Permissions

Symbolic value	Octal Value
Read (r)	4
Write (w)	2
Execute (e)	1

Permissions apply to the user, the group, and to others. Three grouped permissions are allocated to each item for each category.

How to read a **755** or **-rwxr-xr-x** permission

User	Group	Other
rwx	r_x	r_x
4+2+1=7	4+1=5	4+1=5

The Standard Permission

Linux operating systems create files and directories with standard permissions as follows:

Files	666	-rw-rw-rw-
Directories	777	-rwxrwxrwx

The Linux Umask Value

When a Linux user or system administrator create a file or folder, the file and folder are made with a default set of permissions. Generally, these default system permissions are made accessible and loose to enable file sharing. For instance, by default, text files are assigned 666 permissions, which give read and write permissions to everybody. Relatedly a folder or Linux directory has

777 permissions by default, which give read, write, and execute permissions to everybody.

Umask, also called the user file creation mode mask, is a Linux utility employed to determine the file permissions that are assigned to all recently created files. This utility is also utilized to regulate the **default file permissions for all the latest files**. The umask is a quartet or a number that has four digits. A umask can be set or expressed using either symbolic values or Octal values.

The Linux file system umask utility plays an immense responsibility in regulating access authorizations which are allocated to files made and owned by a Linux user. Initially, the umask configuration is that setting which is directly involved in managing the file authorizations assigned during file and folder creation phase. When new files are created through usage of the VI command-line editor or the usage of the touch command-line utility, all the requisite permissions on the files will be assigned from the configured umask setting. Users in Linux can view the configured umask setting merely by keying in the **umask command** on the shell, as shown below:

```
[root@rad-srv ~]# umask
0022
[root@rad-srv ~]#
```

Where the umask Setting comes From

The filesystem umask setting is commonly configured in system-wide files such as the **/etc/profile** file, the **/etc/bashrc file,** and also in the /etc/login.defs file, which is a login file that is utilized when a user logs in. These umask settings are easily overridden through usage of files such as ~/.bashrc and~/.profile, which are user-specific files and are parsed *after all other files have been read* in the later stages of the system login process. The umask setting can also be temporarily reset using the umask command. The illustration below shows

```
[root@rad-srv ~]# grep ^UMASK /etc/login.defs
UMASK         077
[root@rad-srv ~]# umask 002
[root@rad-srv ~]# umask
0002
[root@rad-srv ~]#
```

The major idea of utilizing umask settings is to ensure that we have the desired initial file permissions by default. Linux users can always use the chmod utility on a file, but umask settings remove the need to always using chmod. When the administrator is setting the default file permissions using umask, they decide whether other users in the same group as the file creator or anybody who logs in the Linux system can access and read your files.

Meaning of "mask"

The Linux umask configurations are essentially a reversal of the file permissions they will generate. A digit 0 in a umask may return a 7 for the subsequent permissions, whereas a digit 7 in a umask would yield a digit 0. Consequently, 777 is the most *limiting* umask setting, and 000 is the most liberal.

Below is an illustration of the creation of a new file with the umask setting at 777.

```
[ppeters@rad-srv:~$] umask 777
[ppeters@rad-srv:~$] touch file01
[ppeters@rad-srv:~$] cat file01
cat: file01: Permission denied
[ppeters@rad-srv:~$] ls -l file01
---------- 1 ppeters 0 Nov 12 10:02 file01
[ppeters@rad-srv:~$]
```

The umask setting of 777 is making it impossible to view the file we just created because it is a restrictive setting.

Every bit in file's umask configuration matches to a bit in the file permissions to be utilized. Using chmod the octal 777 signifies rwxrwxrwx, and looking at this in umask it makes the file and folder permissions created to ---------.

In Linux, the umask value of 022 and 002 are the most prevalent settings. The value 022 represents denying write access permissions to users in the owner's group and the universe in the file system, and the umask value 002 represents denying write access permissions to everyone. Nonetheless, the umask value 077 is superior if the administrator intends to deny access to your files by default.

Auxiliary Permissions in Linux
In Linux, the file permissions are the basic level of security. We have basic file permissions covered in the sections above, and we

also what are called special or auxiliary file permissions, which can be set on files and directories. The special file permissions in Linux are, namely, suid, sgid, and sticky bit. The SUID is a supplementary file permission for all executable files, which permits other users to execute the file with applicable permissions of the file owner. In Linux in the place of the typical **x** in the permission symbols, which represents execute permissions, we have symbol s indicating the set user ID or SUID or setuid special file permission for the user. Consequently, the set group ID permission also referred to as the SGID or setgid, applies to executable files and permits other users to inherit the effective GID of file group owner. Similarly, instead of the traditional **x**, which symbolizes execute permissions, we have symbol **s** indicating the SGID auxiliary permissions.

Typically, on Linux operating systems and UNIX variants, file and folder ownership is based on **default uid**called user-id and **defaultgid**commonly referred to as the group-id of the user who created them. The same applies to when a Linux process is started in the operating system: the process operates with the effective user-id and group-id of the user who initiated it, and with the matching privileges. This functionality can be altered through the use of auxiliary permissions.

SUID or setuid Permissions

In Linux, the suid bit is utilized to alter the behavior described above. It's changed so that when an executable is initialized. It does not launch with the rights of the user who started it, but with that of the file owner instead. So, for instance, if an executable has the setuid bit set on it, and it's owned by root, when launched by a normal user, it will operate with root permissions.

Root can give users authorization to execute programs they would usually be unable to. This permission is the SUID permission with a symbolic value **s** or numerical value or octal value **4**.

For example, root can write a C shell script that executes a program and set the SUID of the script with chmod 4777 script or chmod u+s script.

```
[root@rad-srv ~]# chmod 4755 /bin/cat
[root@rad-srv ~]# chmod u+s /bin/grep
[root@rad-srv ~]# ls -l /bin/cat /bin/grep
-rwsr-xr-x 1 root 23260 Oct 30  2019 /bin/cat
-rwsr-xr-x 1 root 85060 Oct 26  2019 /bin/grep
[root@rad-srv ~]#
```

Setting suid Bit

We can set suid bit using two ways, namely, symbolic way and octal value way.

Symbolic Way

```
[root@rad-srv ~]# touch symbolicsuid.txt
[root@rad-srv ~]# ls -l symbolicsuid.txt
-rw-rw-r-- 1 root 0 Nov 12 14:50 symbolicsuid.txt
[root@rad-srv ~]# chmod u+s symbolicsuid.txt
[root@rad-srv ~]# ls -l symbolicsuid.txt
-rwSrw-r-- 1 root 0 Nov 12 14:50 symbolicsuid.txt
[root@rad-srv ~]#
```

Octal or Numeric Way

```
[root@rad-srv ~]# touch octalsuid.txt
[root@rad-srv ~]# ls -l octalsuid.txt
-rw-rw-r-- 1 root 0 Nov 12 14:53 octalsuid.txt
[root@rad-srv ~]# chmod 4655 octalsuid.txt
[root@rad-srv ~]# ls -l octalsuid.txt
-rwSr-xr-x 1 root 0 Nov 12 14:53 octalsuid.txt
[root@rad-srv ~]#
```

SGID or setgid Permissions

The SGID or setgid permission is set for the user group. SGUID has symbolic value **s** and the numeric value of **2**.

Putting SGID permissions on a Linux directory alters the files' group ownership for all files generated in that folder to the directory's group possession. In Linux, we do not require a newgrp command to modify the effective group of the process preceding creation of the file. When the setgid permission bit is set on a Linux directory, all subfolders and regular files generated internally in this folder will have the identical group ownership permissions as their parent directory and not to the user's group ownership.

We also have two ways of setting SGID, that is the symbolic way and the octal way.

SGID the Symbolic Way

```
[root@rad-srv ~]# mkdir sharesgid
[root@rad-srv ~]# ls -ld sharesgid/
drwxrwxr-x 2 root 4096 Nov 12 15:04 sharesgid/
[root@rad-srv ~]# chmod g+s sharesgid/
```

You have mail in /var/spool/mail/root

[root@rad-srv ~]# ls -ld sharesgid/

drwxrwsr-x 2 root 4096 Nov 12 15:04 sharesgid/

[root@rad-srv ~]#

SGID the Octal Way

[root@rad-srv ~]# mkdir folderoctal

[root@rad-srv ~]# ls -ld folderoctal/

drwxrwxr-x 2 root 4096 Nov 12 15:06 folderoctal/

[root@rad-srv ~]# chmod 2775 folderoctal/

[root@rad-srv ~]# ls -ld folderoctal/

drwxrwsr-x 2 root 4096 Nov 12 15:06 folderoctal/

[root@rad-srv ~]#

Sticky Bit

The sticky bit is an auxiliary permission represented by symbol **t** or octal value number 1. The sticky bit permission functions uniquely from suid and sgid we looked at above. The sticky bit does not influence files in the Linux file system; the sticky bit only applies to Linux directories or folders. When the sticky bit is set on a directory in the Linux filesystem, the said folder's will be changeable only by their creators of file owners. A classic instance where sticky bits are used involves the /tmp folder. Classically this /tmp directory is the filesystem hierarchy that can be read and modified by all users on the system. Sticky bits are set to ensure it is difficult for one system user to delete or change files in the /tmp folder that were created by another user.

The sticky bit is principally used to safeguard files inside a directory. Whenever directory has the sticky bit set, a regular file within that folder can only be deleted by file owners, the owner, and creator of the folder and by the system superuser, also called the root user. This is helpful and critical for all openly available folders like /tmp in Linux file systems.

The sticky bit is also configured in two ways, namely symbolic and octal way.

Setting Sticky Bit Symbolic Way

```
[root@rad-srv ~]# mkdir /stickydir
[root@rad-srv ~]# ls -ld /stickydir/
drwxrwxr-x 2 root 4096 Nov 12 15:36 /stickydir/
[root@rad-srv ~]# ls -ld /stickydir/
drwxrwxrwx 2 root 4096 Nov 12 15:36 /stickydir/
[root@rad-srv ~]# chmod +t /stickydir/
[root@rad-srv ~]# ls -ld /stickydir/
drwxrwxrwt 2 root 4096 Nov 12 15:36 /stickydir/
[root@rad-srv ~]#
```

Setting Sticky Bit Octal Way

```
[root@rad-srv ~]# mkdir /stickydiroctal
[root@rad-srv ~]# chmod 1777 /stickydiroctal/
[root@rad-srv ~]# ls -ld /stickydiroctal/
drwxrwxrwt 2 root root 4096 Nov 12 15:38 /stickydiroctal/
[root@rad-srv ~]#
```

Checking if a Folder has the Sticky Bit et

```
[root@rad-srv ~]# ls -ld /tmp/
drwxrwxrwt 5 root root 4096 Nov 12 15:29 /tmp/
[root@rad-srv ~]#
```

In the example above, the directory owner, the group, and everyone have full read, write and execute permissions on the directory. The sticky bit is recognizable by a symbol **t,** which is stated on the executable **x** bit position as displayed above, in the "other or everyone" section. In Linux, a small letter t indicates that the file executable bit is in existence, else we will have capital T.

Input and Output Redirection

Redirection refers to the process of directing input and output to and from files to devices and files other than the normal and standard I/O devices in the shells of the operating system. Usually the standard input typically comes from the keyboard or the mouse, and output goes to the standard results console or display monitor. You may circumvent such settings with a redirecting operator so that a command or script collects input from another device and sent output to another device, console, or file. Each program that is executed from the bash shell starts three files, which are the standard input file, standard output stream, and lastly, the standard error file or stream. These streams or files offer the principal method of interprocess interaction between the programs, and they subsist throughout the process execution. In this same vein, Linux process or program may be directed to where to find input and where to direct and display their output, using *input and output*

81

standard redirection. Linux uses the less than "<" and greater than ">" operators to denote input and output redirection, respectively.

The typical input file affords a process a means to receive data. Fundamentally, the regular input to a process is read from the terminal keyboard. The stdout file descriptor gives Linux processes the outlet for processed data. Primarily process and command results are guided to the shell terminal for displaying. The stderr file descriptor is a conduit for the display of errors arising from command and process execution. Output errors are guided to shell terminal console for display by default.

These Linux built-in redirection capabilities ensure that users are given a set of powerful tools that simplify Linux administration jobs. Usage of input and output file streams can improve the execution of complex system administration tasks through the manipulation of input-output file descriptors.

File Descriptors

Standard Input and the standard output in the Linux is handled through three distinctive file descriptors. These file descriptors are called the **standard input** abbreviated **stdin**, **standard output** abbreviated as **stdout,** and finally, the third descriptor is the **standard error** abbreviated to **stderr**.

In Linux, these standard file descriptors are represented by numbers such as **stdin** symbolized by number zero **(0), while the stdout** fd is denoted by number one **(1),** and finally, the fd **stderr** is denoted by number two **(2)**.

When the user is interacting with the Linux bash terminal, the standard input is conveyed through keystrokes made on the system user's keyboard device. The standard output's file descriptor and standard error file streams are shown on the console terminal as output text. Collectively, the three streams are referred to as the *Linux file descriptors*.

Stdin Stream

The standard input stream commonly moves input text data from the system user's keyboard input to a system or user process. Processes that are awaiting the standard input streams usually get input from an input device, such as a keyboard into the bash terminal. The Linux system accepts input from the keyboard until the Linux prompt reaches the end of the file, which is abbreviated EOF. EOF means that the end of file has been reached as described by the name. This is an indication that the system should not expect any more keyboard input.

Below we are going to display the standard input stream in action. When we want to display the standard input in action, we are going to execute the **cat** utility without any arguments and parameters. The command Cat stands for concatenate, which means to bond or append input text. The **cat** command is regularly employed to conglomerate the contents of two files streams. The cat command starts a circling prompt when used without any options, as shown below by the cursor.

```
[ppeters@rad-srv ~]$ cat
|
```

Typing the cat command opened a prompt waiting for user input. We are going to type in the numbers, as shown below.

```
[ppeters@rad-srv ~]$ cat
123
123
456
456
789
789
[ppeters@rad-srv ~]$
```

From the above illustration, the reader can see that when you enter a digit and press carriage return or enter button, that means you are redirecting the keyboard text input to the executing cat command, which is expecting and awaiting keyboard text input. On entering the text and pressing the enter key, the cat command is relaying your text input back to you as standard output on the terminal console display. That is the reason why we have a double number of rows.

In the instance above, the end of the file was invoked by user input. The user pressing the keyboard combination ctr-d is the EOF equivalent. The cat command terminates after receiving the EOF signal.

Stdout Stream

Linux command-line interface has a display console for expected results of processing and executing Linux commands called the standard output, which is generally shortened to stdout. The stdout stream displays the data created by a Linux program or Linux user process to either the console screen or a determined output file or device. By default, the standard output file descriptor shows its result to the terminal console when not redirected.

Examples to Show stdout Output

The reader should type **echo illustration on the** terminal through standard output

```
[ppeters@rad-srv ~]$ echo illustration
illustration
[ppeters@rad-srv ~]$
```

When we type the echo command with no options, the **echo** command only displays or outputs the argument or parameter statement passed to it. An argument or parameter is the statement that is passed on to a command in the terminal. Fundamentally it is anything that comes after the **command.**

Execute echo without anything such as options and parameters:

```
[ppeters@rad-srv ~]$ echo
[ppeters@rad-srv ~]$
```

The echo command after shows that you get an empty response when you type in the echo program without arguments.

Stderr Stream

In the Linux command line, the stderr or standard error inscribes the error messages generated by a Linux command that failed during execution on the terminal console. The usual target for this stderr error message stream is the terminal console in the command line. When a Linux shell command's stderr is piped to a second command, the piped data, which consists of output errors, is concurrently directed to the shell terminal.

When you execute the cat command on a file stored in a directory without any arguments, you get blank results. Now when you run the cat command on a non-existent file, you are met with an error.

```
[ppeters@rad-srv /]$ cat /etc/div
cat: /etc/div: No such file or directory
[ppeters@rad-srv /]$
```

Since /etc/div directory or file in no there, this results in the standard error stream shown below:

```
cat: /etc/div: No such file or directory
```

Redirection of Input and Output

In the Linux operating system, we have redirection utilities for each stdin, stdout, and stderr file descriptor. These file streams redirect their standard outcomes to a file. If we specify a non-existent file through usage of a single bracket or usage of a double bracket command, a new file is generated that has the name specified in the single or double bracket command. All Linux commands that are written with a single bracket *overwrite* the present contents of the targeted directory.

Symbols that Overwrite

The single symbol for stdout, this greater than sign > overwrites the content of the file they are executing on. The less than sign, which is a sign for stdin or standard input, also overwrites as does the 2> symbol for standard error.

All Linux commands specified with double-brackets *don't* overwrite the target file's current contents. The double symbols only add or append to the contents of a specified file. The >>, << and 2>> symbols for standard output, input, and error respectively result in the contents of a target file being added to or appended to.

Redirection Examples

```
[ppeters@rad-srv ~]$ cat > redirect.txt
we
are
the
best
ctrl-d
```

The results of the cat command above can be viewed below using the cat redirect.txt command.

```
[ppeters@rad-srv ~]$ cat redirect.txt
we
are
the
best
[ppeters@rad-srv ~]$
```

As shown above, the cat command is being used to write to a file, which is created as a result of the loop.

Redirect cat to write*to*me.txt again, and enter three numbers.

```
[ppeters@rad-srv ~]$ cat > redirect.txt
1
2
3
ctrl-d
[ppeters@rad-srv ~]$
```

Now viewing the contents of the redirect.txt file using the cat redirect.txt command, the output is as follows:

```
[ppeters@rad-srv ~]$ cat redirect.txt
1
2
3
[ppeters@rad-srv ~]$
```

Looking at the results above, we see that the redirect.txt file contents have been overwritten and replaced by numbers instead of the words.

Do one more cat redirection, this time using double brackets:

```
[ppeters@rad-srv ~]$ cat >> redirect.txt
This
is
appended
```

```
ctrl-d
[ppeters@rad-srv ~]$
```

After typing the command cat >> redirect.txt the result will be as follows:

```
[ppeters@rad-srv ~]$ cat redirect.txt
1
2
3
This
is
appended
[ppeters@rad-srv ~]$
```

The above file redirect.txt now includes text from the two cat > redirect.txt and cat >> redirect.txt, the command using the >> symbol just added its text to the redirect.txt.

Linux Piping

Pipes can redirect a stdin, stdout, and stderr stream from one program to the other. The data received by the second program will not be displayed on the terminal if the default program output is sent via a pipe to another program. The second The *pipe symbol* is denoted by the vertical bar "|."

Illustration of using pipes in Linux:

```
[root@mx3 ~]# cat /etc/rc.local | more
```

The example above takes the resulting output of the cat /etc/rc.local command, which shows the contents of the rc.local file, and *piping* the output of this command to the *more* command. The more command shows the data sent to it one screen at a time.

However the operation of the Linux pipe can seem to be related to that of the stdout > and >> redirects, the difference is that piping relays data from one program to the next, while the stdout redirection operators ">" and " >>" are mainly utilized to redirect singularly to Linux files.

Filters

In the Linux operating system, we use filters to alter piped redirection and output operators. Please note that filter programs are also regular Linux directives that can also be utilized without pipes. The first filter is the **find** command, which displays files with filenames that are equivalent to the parameter string or find string passed to find. The second filter we have is the **grep** command, which essentially yields text that equals the search pattern string passed to the grep command. The third command we will look at is the tee program, which is used to redirect standard input to both standard output and one or more Linux files. The fourth filter is the tr command, which primarily is used to find and replace strings with other strings. Lastly, we can also use the command **wc**, which counts characters, lines, and words as a filter with Linux piping.

Illustration of Piping

We are going to see piping, redirection and filters in action in this section of the chapter. The command below redirects its output to redirection_file.txt.

command > redirection_file.txt

```
[ppeters@rad-srv ~]$ ls -l / > ls_redirect.txt
[ppeters@rad-srv ~]$ cat ls_redirect.txt
total 98
dr-xr-xr-x.   2 root root  4096 Jul 30 11:18 bin
dr-xr-xr-x.   5 root root  1024 Jul 30 11:18 boot
drwxr-xr-x.  17 root root  3640 Nov 17 18:00 dev
drwxr-xr-x.  71 root root  4096 Nov 17 18:00 etc
drwxr-xr-x.  14 root root  4096 Apr  5  2016 home
dr-xr-xr-x.  10 root root  4096 Jul 30 11:17 lib
dr-xr-xr-x.   9 root root 12288 Jul 30 11:18 lib64
drwx------.   2 root root 16384 Sep 19  2013 lost+found
drwxr-xr-x.   2 root root  4096 Sep 23  2011 media
drwxr-xr-x.   2 root root  4096 Sep 23  2011 mnt
```

The above ls -l command above passes the long listing output result of the root folder as standard output and inserts the result to ls_redirection.txt file. Since this is a single bracket command, it is going to overwrite the contents of the ls_redirect.txt file if it is not empty.

command > /dev/null

The file **/dev/null** is a peculiar or special Linux file utilized to make trash from any records that are sent to it. This /dev/null file is used to throw away any standard output that is not required, and that may then mess with the operations of a Linux command or a bash script. All system and command output that is redirected to the /dev/null file is rejected and thrown away into the garbage or trash in the Linux system.

```
[ppeters@smtp ~]$ ls / > /dev/null
[ppeters@smtp ~]$
```

This command above does away with the standard output file stream sent from the command *ls /* by sending it to /dev/null file.

command 2> stderr_file

The command above redirects the stderr or standard error file stream to the file called stderr_file, overwriting any existing text contents in the stderr_file if it is not empty.

```
[ppeters@smtp ~]$ mkdir " 2> stderr_file.txt
[ppeters@smtp ~]$ cat stderr_file.txt
mkdir: cannot create directory '': No such file or directory
[ppeters@smtp ~]$
```

The command above redirects the mkdir error returned from the above command and writes it to stderr_file.txt. Please do note that the stderr message is still sent to the display terminal and shown as text.

command >> file

This command above redirects the stdout or standard output of an executed command to a specified file *without* writing over the present contents of the file.

```
[ppeters@smtp    ~]$    echo    "Contents    overwritten"    >
ls_redirect.txt
[ppeters@smtp ~]$ cat ls_redirect.txt
Contents overwritten
[ppeters@smtp ~]$
```

```
[ppeters@smtp ~]$ echo "We have appended to the above" >>
ls_redirect.txt
[ppeters@smtp ~]$ cat ls_redirect.txt
Contents overwritten
We have appended to the above
[ppeters@smtp ~]
```

With the pair of commands above, the first command redirects the text inputted by the user through echo to the ls_redirect.txt file, this command overwrites the ls contents which were put in the file earlier. The second command using the double greater than symbol adds the content to the next line of the ls_redirect.txt file without overwriting its contents.

command 2>> file

The command above merely redirects the stderr also known as the standard error text from the command to a file *without* writing over the preexisting contents in the file. The command for standard error is more beneficial in the creation of error logs for a commands, processes and Linux services. This command will ensure that previous logs already in the file are not cleared off but we just add more to the logs.

```
[ppeters@smtp ~]$ find " 2> stderr_logfile.txt
[ppeters@smtp ~]$ ls
ls_redirect.txt redirect.txt stderr_file.txt stderr_logfile.txt
[ppeters@smtp ~]$ cat stderr_logfile.txt
find: cannot search `": No such file or directory
[ppeters@smtp ~]$
```

Example to append to error log

```
[ppeters@smtp ~]$ wc " 2>> stderr_logfile.txt
[ppeters@smtp ~]$ cat stderr_logfile.txt
find: cannot search `': No such file or directory
wc: invalid zero-length file name
[ppeters@smtp ~]$
```

The above two commands redirect the Linux file system error messages thrown by an invalid find command parameter to a file named stderr_logfile.txt. The second example command then adds to the next line, the **wc** error thrown by an invalid wc parameter to the stderr_logfile.txt file.

command | command

The vertical line above is called the pipe and it redirects the stdout also known as the standard output from the primary command to the standard input of the subsequent command.

```
[root@mx3 ~]# find /var zone | grep uz
/var/spool/postfix/flush/science_uz_ac_zw
/var/spool/postfix/flush/medic_uz_ac_zw
/var/spool/postfix/flush/compcentre_uz_ac_zw
/var/spool/postfix/flush/medsch_uz_ac_zw
/var/spool/postfix/flush/cs_uz_ac_zw
/var/spool/postfix/flush/students_uz_ac_zw
/var/spool/postfix/flush/vet_uz_ac_zw
/var/spool/postfix/flush/sociol_uz_ac_zw
/var/spool/postfix/flush/agric_uz_ac_zw
/var/spool/postfix/flush/eng_uz_ac_zw
```

```
/var/spool/postfix/flush/sifeuz_uz_ac_zw
/var/spool/postfix/flush/commerce_uz_ac_zw
/var/spool/postfix/flush/uzlib_uz_ac_zw
/var/spool/postfix/flush/admin_uz_ac_zw
```

[root@mx3 ~]#

The above command searches through /var and its subdirectories for files and extensions that match the string *uz* and returns the file paths for the files, with the identical portion in each path emphasized.

command | tee file

This command, which comprises the *tee* command, is used to redirect the Linux command's standard output to a file while overwriting the contents of the said file. The command then shows the transmitted output in the shell terminal. It generates a new file that is not already in existence.

From the perspective of this command, tee is classically used to envision a command's output while concurrently saving it to a file.

```
[ppeters@smtp ~]$ wc /etc/magic | tee tee_count.txt
 3  19 111 /etc/magic
[ppeters@smtp ~]$
```

The command above pipes the totals for characters, lines, and words in the /etc/magic file to the tee command, which then breakups the wc's result in two ways, and directs it to the console display and the tee_count.txt file.

In Linux, we can use several pipes to redirect output across numerous commands and/or filters.

command | command | command >> file

The command above redirects the standard output of the first command and filters it across the next double commands. The above statement then attaches the finishing output to a Linux file.

[root@mx3 ~]# ls / | grep *tar | tr e E >> ls_logfile.txt

The command above starts by executing the ls command in your root directory (/), and the output is piped to the grep command. The grep yields a listing of files, including *tar* extension or the string tar in their name.

The resulting output from grep command is subsequently piped to tr command, which replaces incidences of the letter *e* with *E*, since e is being passed as the first parameter which is the pattern string we are searching for, and letter E is passed as the second parameter which in this case is the string that swaps any equivalents for the first parameter. The final output from the command is then added to the file ls_logfile.txt, which is created if it does not already exist.

Conclusion

The training to use the redirecting functionality embedded into the command line may be a little bit overwhelming, but after concluding this section of the book, you are well on the path to understanding this skill. Currently, since you've understood the basics of how input/output redirections, filters, and pipes work, you may persist with your expedition into the bash shell scripting ecosystem, which repeatedly uses the commands and statements summarized in this section of the book.

Chapter 4

VI Command Line Editor

---◦◆◦---

This "**vi**" section of the book is intended for those who wish to master and advance their skills beyond the basic features of the basic editor as covered in "The Linux Command Line" book. It includes buffers, "**vi**" command-line instructions, interfacing with UNIX commands, and ctags. The **vim** editor is an enhanced version of **vi**. The improvements are noticed in the handling of tags.

Introduction

VI is a potent and universal shell or command line text editor that is available by default in most Linux distributions and many other operating systems such as Windows OS and the macOS. It is common knowledge that the command line is text input and output only Linux console. All Linux System Administrators must have basic knowledge of the vi text editor. vi, pronounced like 'vee eye,' was initially created by Bill Joy for the operating system called BSD Unix.

Vi stands for *visual editor,* and this text file manipulation tool is a large enhancement to the traditional and old Unix editor named **ed**. The vi command-line editor has mainly two modes of operation, which are the line-mode, called **ex,** and the regular multi-line mode we are discussing. Indeed, some people may debate that this text editor is two text editors folded into one, one of the editors called vi, and the other one called ex. When working with the VI editor, it is feasible to shift between line and visual mode throughout the editing session. Users may choose the operating mode they prefer during startup. Though, pure usage of the line-editor **ex** is rare. The vi editor's visual operation mode is the predominant mode. Although vi stands for the *visual editor*, this classic editor is mainly operated via keyboard character keys, and not via the mouse or the cursor keys. The usage of characters for proficient users make it extremely useful since there is less movement of the hands-on cursor keys or mouse.

The benefit of studying the **vi editor** and understanding it sufficiently well is that one will find **vi** on all Linux distributions and many other Unix systems and their variant systems. VI text editor does not use an excessive quantity of Computer system hardware and processing resources. Vi works great over slow networks like some VPN modem connections and on computers with limited computation resources.

VI or VIM Editor Installation

Red Hat / CentOS / Fedora

```
[ppeters@rad-srv ~]$ rpm -ivh vim-common-...rpm vim-minimal-...rpm vim-enhanced-...rpm vim-X11-...rpm
```

Using Yum package Manager:

```
[ppeters@rad-srv ~]$ yum install vim-common vim-minimal vim-enhanced vim-X11
```

Ubuntu / Debian

```
[ppeters@rad-srv ~]$ apt-get install vim vim-common vim-
gnome vim-gui-common vim-runtime
```

Compiling Vim from source:

Download vim source from http://vim.org

```
[ppeters@rad-srv ~]$ wget ftp://ftp.vim.org/pub/vim/unix/vim-
8.1.tar.bz2
[ppeters@rad-srv ~]$ tar xvjf vim-8.1.tar.bz2
[ppeters@rad-srv ~]$ cd vim81
[ppeters@rad-srv ~]$ ./configure –prefix=/opt –enable-cscope
[ppeters@rad-srv ~]$ make
[ppeters@rad-srv ~]$ make install
```

VI text Editor Features

Vi text editor is called a *modal* **command line text** editor which operates in unique operating modes. The vi text editor can take a Linux command.

Users can manipulate text and data contained in files using the vi command line text editor, by putting this vi text editor into an operation mode. You enter the vi text editor's command operation mode whenever you desire to send program commands to the vi text editor. It is the default operation mode for the editor. When the administrator wants to edit or enter new text into a text or script file, they have to invoke the Insert Mode by pressing the letter I on the keyboard. The incoming section of the book covers the vi text editor's Insertion Mode. The very opening time you decide to start the vi command-line editor, it instinctively starts in the operation mode called the command mode.

Insertion Mode

When the user wants to edit and to enter new text in a file, we need to operate and get the vi text editor into an operation mode called the **Insert mode**. When the vi command line text editor is opened, it always initializes in an operation sphere called the **command mode**. To enable insertion into the file press keyboard's i key or button to convert from Command mode into *insert mode*, and it is in this mode that you able to start typing. The backspace key is used to resolve the errors you make. To exit the editor's insert mode after you're finished typing, and return to command mode, you press the Escape key on your keyboard (or type Control-[ ).

The basic way of entering text into a file using the VI editor is by typing the command below:

[ppeters@rad-srv ~]$ vi file_name.txt

The example above shows the VI text editor command usage on the file called file_name.txt. If the file_name.txt is blank, you get the result below:

~

~

~

~

~

~

101

```
~
~
"file_name.txt" [New File]          0,0-1        All
```

On the screen above, we get to choose the mode you would like to work in the text editor.

The vi editor has three modes, namely the command, insert, and the last-line mode. These modes determine the activities that can be done on the file. The first mode you get to when you type vi file_name.txt is called the command mode. In this mode, the user can select their working or operation mode by typing some key or entering a symbol. Typing the letter or character **"i"** gets you into Insert Mode.

VI Command mode: When we initialize the **vi** command-line editor, it gets into the Command Mode. It is in this mode that the vi text editor processes and decodes any characters typed on its console as commands; hence, it does not display them in the console. This mode allows us to traverse through a file and to erase, duplicate and paste some text. For any user to get into the vi text editor Command Mode from any mode, the user needs to press the keyboard **Esc** key. If we press [Esc] when we are already in Command Mode, then vi will beep or flash the screen.

VI Insert mode: This vi text editor mode enables you to insert text into a file in the filesystem. All that a user types when in this text editing mode is assumed as input text that is eventually added to the file. The vi text editor forever begins in command mode. To enter text, you must be in insert mode. To come in insert mode, you type the letter **i** on the keyboard. To get out of insert mode, press the Esc key, which will put you back into command mode.

VI Last-line mode: The vi editor's last Line Mode is reached when a user types the full colon **(:) on the vi editor command mode**. The terminal's cursor moves to the last line of the vi editor screen and waits for user input, which is treated as a command. It is in this mode that we can perform jobs like saving files and running Linux commands.

Example of vi text editor command:

```
[root@rad-srv ~]#
[root@rad-srv ~]# vi /etc/rc.local
```

And below is the result of the command

```
#!/bin/sh
#
# This script will be executed *after* all the other init scripts.
# You can put your own initialization stuff in here if you don't
# want to do the full Sys V style init stuff.

touch /var/lock/subsys/local
#route add -net 10.0.0.0/8 dev eth0
route add -net 10.0.0.0/8 gw 10.50.1.1
```

```
#route add -net 10.20.0.0/16 gw 172.16.0.1
#route add -net 10.200.0.0/16 dev eth0
route add -net 10.200.0.0/16 gw 10.200.1.1
#/usr/lib/openoffice.org3/program/soffice                    "-
accept=socket,host=localhost,port=8100;urp;StarOffice.Service
Manager" -nologo -headless -nofirststartwizard &
ntpdate -u 10.17.2.1
service mysqld start
service clamd start
service amavisd start
service dovecot start
service postfix start
~
~
~
"/etc/rc.local" 19L, 702C
```

VI Text Editor Movement of the Cursor

Vi Keys	Expected Action
h/j/k/l	These keys are used to move the cursor to the left, down, up and lastly to the right
spacebar	Pressing the spacebar moves cursor one space to the right
-/+	Move cursor down/up in the first column
ctrl-d	These keys are used to Scroll down one half of a page
ctrl-u	These keys are used to Scroll up one half of a page

ctrl-f	These keys are used to Scroll forward one page
ctrl-b	These keys are used to Scroll back one page
M (shift-h)	These keys are used to Move the cursor to the middle of the page
H	The key moves the cursor to the top of page
L	The key moves the cursor to bottom of page
W	The key moves the cursor a word at a time
w	The key moves the cursor ahead 5 words
5w	
B	The key moves the cursor back a word at a time
b	The key moves the cursor back a word at a time
5b	The key moves the cursor back 5 words
e	The key moves the cursor to the end of the word
5e	The key moves the cursor ahead to the end of the 5th word
0 (zero)	The key moves the cursor to the beginning of the line
$	The key moves the cursor to the end of line
)	The key moves the cursor to the beginning of next sentence
(	The key moves the cursor to the beginning of the current sentence
G	The key moves the cursor to end of file
%	The key moves the cursor to the matching bracket. Place cursor on {}[]() and type "%". Use the matchit or xmledit plug-in to extend this

	capability to XML/XHTML tags.
'.	The key moves the cursor to the previously modified line.
'a	The key moves the cursor to line mark "a" generated by marking with keystroke "ma"
'A	The key moves the cursor to line mark "a" (global between buffers) generated by marking with keystroke "mA"
]'	Move the cursor to the next lower case mark.
['	Move the cursor to the previous lower case mark.

Editing commands:

Keystrokes	Action
I	This key permits a user to Insert at the location of cursor
A	opens vi editor in Insert mode to add text next to the cursor
A	Add text to the end of the line indicated by the cursor
ESC	Exit Insert mode and get into Command mode
U	Undo the last change you made
U	Undo all the changes made on the whole line
O	Open vi editor and start a new line to insert text

dd	Delete just a single line
6dd	Delete six lines from the cursor position going down
D	Delete all the contents of line coming after the cursor
C	Delete all the contents in a line after the cursor and start inserting new text. To terminate the insertion, press the ESC key.
dw	Use this to delete a word
6dw	Use this to delete six words
Cw	Alter the word
X	Delete only a character at position of cursor
R	Replace a character on cursor position
R	Overwrite characters from cursor onward
S	Substitute one character under cursor continue to insert
S	Substitute the line and start at the beginning of the line
~	Change the case of an individual character
ctrl-a	Increment number under the cursor.
ctrl-x	Decrement number under the cursor.
/search_string{CR}	Search for *search_string and press enter key*

?search_string{CR}	Search backwards (up in file) for *search_string*
∧<search_string\>{CR}	Search for *search_word*
	Ex: ∧<s\>
	Search for the variable "s" but ignore declaration "string" or words containing "s". This will find "string s;", "s = fn(x);", "x = fn(s);", etc
N	Find the next occurrence of search_word
N	Find the previous occurrence of search_word
.	repeat last command action.

Closing a VI Text Editor Session

There are several ways to terminate a vi editor session. The first one is the usage of the command ZZ. This ZZ command saves all the changes made to the file and then quits the text editor. We can also use the vi text editor command **(wq),** which writes changes we have made and also quits the vi command-line editor. The other commands that we can type in the vi Command Mode are "w," which writes the changes we have made without exiting the editor. To quit the editor after making a save, we use the **"q"** command. Lastly, we can also use the "qa" command to quit all files open in the vi editor.

Deleting

If you have made a mistake after a few lines, for instance, pressing the Backspace key until the mistake is gone and starting again isn't always the best solution. We need a method of deleting mistakes that happen in the normal course of editing. Vi allows you several methods of deleting text, based on how much needs to be removed. Now that you are familiar with moving around, once you've moved the cursor to where the error is by pressing the x key deletes only *one* character at the cursor position while pressing the duo dw deletes *a single* word also at the cursor and lastly pressing the letter combination dd only deletes *one* line

Purpose description	Vi command
Get into insert mode and enter text	Press ESC + i, escape key then press i
Saving a file	**ESC + : + w** the user presses the 'ESC' key then type full colon and finally type 'w')
Saving a file with name file_name	**ESC + : + w "file_name"** Press ESC key and type w and specify filename
Quitting the vi text editor	**ESC + : + q** Press the ESC key, then a colon and lastly letter q
Quitting an edited file without saving	**ESC + : + q!** Press ESC key then a full colon, followed by letter q and exclamation mark to force the quitting

Save and quit after editing a file	**Esc + : + wq** Press the ESC key, then a full colon, and type the two letters wq. W for write and q for quit
Searching for the indicated term in a forward focus direction (From cursor to the end of file)	**ESC + /word_to_search** Initially Press 'ESC' key, then type /search-string, to locate a string name you type /named on the command console. A single search is done here.
To go on ahead, searching for occurrences of the string	Press N on your keyboard
To find an indicated word in the backward focus direction (from the end of file up)	**ESC + ?search_string** First press the 'ESC' key, type the word to search
Yanking or copying a line	**ESC + yy** This copies the cursor indicated line
Pasting the copied or deleted text at the cursor location	**Esc + p** Press the ESC key and type p
Deleting a whole line at the cursor location	**ESC + dd**
Deleting a word at the cursor location	**ESC + dw**

Finding and replacing words in the whole file	esc + :$s/search_word/replace_word/g For. e.g. :$s/salisbury/harare/g Here the word "salisbury" is replaced with the word "harare."
Finding and replacing word in a file globally and making confirmations	esc + :$s/search_word/replace_word/cg
Executing bash shell commands like **ls**, **cp**, and **date** on the vi editor prompt	ESC + :!bash_command Press the ESC key to get into command mode then type a full colon followed by an exclamation mark and the command For example :!date

Advanced VI Text Editor

Every vi text editor row can be marked to ensure we can come back to the row faster when needed. To mark a row, all we have to do is type the letter **m** and any extra character to mark the actual text line. Users can reference the marked row by typing a text string that comprises of "'" and additional letter meant for identifying the text row. For example, typing the letter combination **mf** will mark a vi text editor line and identify it using letter **f**. Pressing the string "'**f**" will take the text editor's cursor to the row, which we marked using the character **f**. It is possible to mark some lines as a block of text.

This block of lines is referenced to by the starting marker and the ending marker, for example, we can mark row with **f** and mark the ending of the block of lines with letter **s** such that we can reference the whole block of lines by string **'f,'s.**

VI Yanking

In vi command line text editor, we can copy lines of text into the memory buffer by a process called yanking. Yanking is done through typing double letter y as **yy**, we can also use y for yanking with a combination of other characters such as **y't** and **#yy** where the hash symbol # stands for a number. We can use "**yy**" to yank or copy a single-line text that is demarcated by the present cursor spot into the buffer. We can also use the "**y't**" combination to yank text from present cursor spot to the line marked "t," this command is used to copy multiple lines of text in the vi cditor. Lastly, we can copy or yank several lines by prefixing our double ys with a number. For example, "**4yy**" is used to yank four lines meaning the existing line and three more lines beneath it.

Copying from the Buffer in VI Editor

We use the letter "**p**" to place contents of stored in the buffer through yanking, and this text is placed after the current line demarcated by the cursor location.

Moving Text Blocks

In the vi text editor, it is feasible to move text blocks to the left or the right. The requirement for you to be able to do this is to get into VI's **visual mode** through pressing character **v** at the uppermost or lowermost section of your text block, which you need to move.

After getting into visual mode, the subsequent phase is to move the cursor to the bottom or upper portion of your text block using of characters j and k or use the keyboard arrow keys. It is logical to pick from the initial column starting from the upper line and the final character at the line that is found at the bottom line. Pressing the Zero (0) digit on the keyboard moves the cursor to the first or initial symbol in that line. Pressing the dollar symbol $ moves the cursor to the last character in that line. Using the double greater than sign (>>) moves the text block rightwards while using the double less-than sign (<<) shifts the text block leftwards. Please note that the shift width setting determines the size of the characters moved. For instance 9: ":set sw=9". The setting here means that we are setting the shift width to 9 characters.

VI Command Mode

The vi text editor operates in the command mode by default. The vi command mode can be accessed through the usage of the full colon :. Users can leave the command mode by pressing the enter key. We have example commands we can type in the Command mode, as shown below.

The example command below is used to display line numbers in the text file we are working with in the vi editor.

:set number

If we are not sure about the full name of a particular command in the vi text editor command mode, we can use TAB completion within our vi editor to help completing the name of the command.

Pressing **Ctrl-D** displays the whole list of probable names of commands in the vi editor. We have examples of command like the **:set all** which shows all settings of the current user session. The next example we are looking at is the **:set ic** command which alters the vi editor settings so that they ignore the case of letters or characters for all the text searches to be made on the command line console of the vi editor. The default setting is altered from noignorecase to ignorecase. In the example above, the word, **ic** represents the phrase **set ignorecase**.

Set Command Switches

abbreviation	The option	Explanation
ai or noai	autoindent or noautoindent	Allow indentation or not
aw or noaw	autowrite or noautowrite	Permit autowriting or not
eb or noeb	errorbells or noerrorbells	Let bells chime when there's errors
fl or nofl	flash or noflash	Make your screen flash or not when an error occurs, meant for deaf people
ts	tabstop=5	Tab stop setting allows display of specific tabs
ic or noic	Ignorecase or noignorecase	Toggle case sensitivity of searches
nu or nonu	number or nonumber	This toggles on line numbers in the editor

	showmatch or noshowmatch	Permits the vi editor to show matching ")" & "}" symbols
	showmode or noshowmode	This toggles display of editor mode
tl	taglength	Default=0. Set significant characters
	closepunct="'.,;)]}	% key shows matching symbol. Also, see showmatch
	linelimit=32768	Max file size to permitted to edit
ws or nows	wrapscan or nowrapscan	Split up long lines when the option is on
wm or nowm	wrapmargin=0 or nowrapmargin	Configure the rightmost margin for line enveloping.
	list or nolist	Display all Tabs/Ends of lines.
	bg=dark bg=light	Use the option to pick the color pattern for a "dark" or "light" terminal background.

Search and Replacing Patterns

In vi editor, since we are dealing with text files, we may want to search through a large configuration text file for some text patterns and in turn, make replacements for some search patterns. We are going to be using the searchandreplace.txt file to demonstrate the search and replace below.

```
[root@mx3 ~]# vi searchandreplace.txt

[root@mx3 ~]# cat searchandreplace.txt
We are were we are because we are great

We are were we are because we are great

We are were we are because we are great

Were we are is where we ought to be.

This is the best that is for us all

Are you sure this is your main goal
We are were we are because we are great
We are were we are because we are great
We are were we are because we are great

Are you sure this is your main goal
Are you sure this is your main goal
Are you sure this is your main goal
```

Are you sure this is your main goal

Are you sure this is your main goal

Are you sure this is your main goal

[root@mx3 ~]#

This command **:%s/are/is/** searches for the occurrence of the text string **are** all text rows in a file and substitute the search string with **"is"** for the first occurrence only.

Before executing the command

We are were we are because we are great

We are were we are because we are great

We are were we are because we are great

Were we are is where we ought to be.

This is the best that is for us all

Are you sure this is your main goal
We are were we are because we are great
We are were we are because we are great
We are were we are because we are great

Are you sure this is your main goal
Are you sure this is your main goal

```
Are you sure this is your main goal
Are you sure this is your main goal
Are you sure this is your main goal
Are you sure this is your main goal


~

~

:%s/are/is/
```

After Executing the Command

We is were we are because we are great

We is were we are because we are great

We is were we are because we are great

Were we is is where we ought to be.

This is the best that is for us all

Are you sure this is your main goal
We is were we are because we are great
We is were we are because we are great
We is were we are because we are great

Are you sure this is your main goal
Are you sure this is your main goal
Are you sure this is your main goal

Are you sure this is your main goal

Are you sure this is your main goal

Are you sure this is your main goal

~

~

7 substitutions on 7 lines

This search command **:%s/were/where/g** looks for occurrences of the word were in all the rows of the file and substitutes the string results with the **"where"** for every instance in the file.

Before Executing the Command for Search and Replace

We are were we are because we are great

We are were we are because we are great

We are were we are because we are great

Were we are is where we ought to be.

This is the best that is for us all

Are you sure this is your main goal
We are were we are because we are great
We are were we are because we are great
We are were we are because we are great

Are you sure this is your main goal

```
Are you sure this is your main goal
Are you sure this is your main goal
Are you sure this is your main goal
Are you sure this is your main goal
Are you sure this is your main goal


~

~

:%s/were/where/g
```

After Execution of the Command

```
We are where we are because we are great

We are where we are because we are great

We are where we are because we are great

Were we are is where we ought to be.

This is the best that is for us all

Are you sure this is your main goal
We are where we are because we are great
We are where we are because we are great
We are where we are because we are great

Are you sure this is your main goal
Are you sure this is your main goal
```

Are you sure this is your main goal
Are you sure this is your main goal
Are you sure this is your main goal
Are you sure this is your main goal

~

~

6 substitutions on 6 lines

This search command **:%s/were/where/gc** is used to traverse a text file, looking for all occurrences of the word "**were**" and replace with the string **"where"** for each instance in the text file and will also prompt for confirmation.

We are were we are because we are great

We are were we are because we are great

We are were we are because we are great

Were we are is where we ought to be.

This is the best that is for us all

Are you sure this is your main goal
We are were we are because we are great
We are were we are because we are great
We are were we are because we are great
Are you sure this is your main goal

```
Are you sure this is your main goal
Are you sure this is your main goal
Are you sure this is your main goal
Are you sure this is your main goal
Are you sure this is your main goal


~

~
```

replace with where (y/n/a/q/l/^E/^Y)?

This search command **:%s/what/that/gi** looks for all occurrences of the string **"what"** in the text file, and replace with string "that" for every instance of **"what."** This search is very case insensitive meaning it ignores letter case.

This search command here **:'v,'zs/were/where/gi** searches for all the lines between line marked "v" (mv) and line marked "z" (mz), looking for string **"what"** and replace that string with **"that"** for each instance on a line and in the file. This is very case insensitive.

This command here **:%s/*$/** also searches for all lines in a file, deletes all the blank spaces at the end of each line.

This command :%s/\(.*\):\(.*\)/\2:\1/g looks for all lines in a file and shifts the last column bounded by full colon ":" to the first column. This results in a swap of fields if the file has only two columns.

The Linux vi text editor provides us some techniques to find additional details and gain an understanding in the vi text editor through usage of the commands like **:help substitute, :help pattern, :help gdefault, and lastly :help cmdline-ranges.**

Vi Editor Text Sorting

In Linux, we can sort text files using the Vi text editor. The initial step when sorting text files is to mark our text blocks starting at the first line and setting the bottommost line of the block of text. i.e., "**mv**" and "**mz**" on two detached lines. This text block is then referenced by using the combination "'**v,'z**. in our example or using the command **:'v,'z.**

Vi Editor and Awk

In vi editor, we can make use of this command **:'v,. !awk '{print $4 " " $3 " " $2}'** to reverse the course of the fields in our text block. The text block is outlined here as from the line marked with the keystroke **(vz)** and the current line denoted by dot **(.).** This text block is referenced as "'**v,.**". As an example, the text string **aaa bbb ccc ddd** transforms to **aaa ddd ccc bbb**, while **vvv xxx yyy zzz** becomes this **vvv zzz yyy xxx** and lastly **000 111 222 333** changes to   **000 333 222 111.** The example above switches column 4,3 and 2

Working on Multiple Files

Vi editor permits the user to edit more than one file

```
[root@mx3 ~]# vi mfile01 mfile02 mfile03
3 files to edit
[root@mx3 ~]#

~

~
```

```
~

~

~

"mfile01" [New File]



~

~

~

~

"mfile02" [New] 1L, 16C written
E173: 1 more file to edit
Press ENTER or type command to continue
```

When you are in the multiple file mode, you type command :n so that you move to edit the next file mfile02 in our case. After editing file mfile01 and then file mfile02, you can press ESC and type command **:n** to get into the third file mfile03 for work in there as well. We can also move backward from file mfile03 using the command **:rew which essentially means to rewind.**

Chapter 5

Process Management

————————◆◆————————

Aprocess in Linux denotes a program being run on a filesystem; it is a running occurrence of a program. It comprises instructions for the program, data from files, other programs, or system user input.

Process Types

There are fundamentally two types of processes in Linux, namely foreground and background processes. Linux foreground processes are also known as interactive processes. These processes are primed and organized through a command line terminal session. Foreground processes require a user to be connected to the system to initialize them. These processes do not start automatically as part of the system startup services or tasks.

In the same vein, Background processes are known as non-interactive or automatic processes. These are processes that are not associated with a shell terminal, and they do not anticipate user input in their system lifetime.

What are Daemons

In Linux, Daemons are a special or auxiliary type of process that runs in the background and is initialized at system bootup.

Daemons continue executing or running persistently as a Linux service. In Linux OS, daemons are started as system tasks, and they run as system services naturally. Nevertheless, daemons can be coordinated by the system administrator or Linux user through the system INIT process.

Process Creation in Linux

In Linux, new processes are ordinarily produced when a current process creates a precise duplicate of itself in the system memory. This newly created child process will operate in the environment similar to that of its parent, albeit with a unique number called the process ID.

We have two established methods for creating new processes in Linux, such as using the System() Function and usage of fork() and exec () functions. Working with the Linux System () function is moderately simple. Nonetheless, this method is inefficient and has considerably definite security risks.

The method of using fork () and exec () functions is more sophisticated but provides more elasticity, quickness, jointly with security.

Identifying Processes in Linux

Linux is a multi-user operating system, which means that we have distinctive users controlling several programs on this system with every executing instance of a program requiring to be uniquely identified by the Linux kernel.

Every process, task, or running program in Linux is classified and recognized by its process identifier which is abbreviated PID. Their parent processes also identify processes. Identifier also abbreviated PPID. Linux processes are furthermore categorized into parent and child processes. Parent processes are those processes that spawn other processes throughout system run-time. On the other hand, Child process are those processes which are born or created from and by other parent processes during run-time.

The Init Process

The Linux Init process is the parent or initiator or creator of all the other processes on the Linux operating system. The Init process is the foremost program to be executed during the Linux boot process. This parent process administers all the other processes on our Linux system. The Init process is started by the Linux kernel, which principally means it has no parent process. The process ID or PID of the init process is always number 1. The Init process works as the adoptive mother for every orphaned process. Some command-line utilities are used to manage Linux Processes.

The **pidof** command is used to find the PID of a process on the Linux terminal:

```
[root@rad-srv ~]# pidof init
1
[root@rad-srv ~]# pidof dovecot
10955
[root@rad-srv ~]# pidof smtpd
20305 19405 19396 19359
```

```
[root@rad-srv ~]#
```

Finding Linux Process ID

To find the process ID and parent process ID of the current shell, run:

```
[root@rad-srv ~]# echo $$
20696
[root@rad-srv ~]# echo $PPID
20694
[root@rad-srv ~]#
```

Find Linux Parent Process ID

Starting a Process in Linux

Once you run a command or program, for instance, tar command which is the CloudCommander, a process is started within the system. An administrator or Linux user can start an interactive or foreground process as shown below, it will be connected to the terminal, and a user can send input it:

```
[root@rad-srv ~]# tar -czf home.tar.gz.

[2]+  Stopped            tar -czf home.tar.gz.
[root@rad-srv ~]# bg
[2]+ tar -czf home.tar.gz . &
[root@rad-srv ~]#
```

Linux Background Jobs

To start a process in the background or the non-interactive mode, we use the ampersand **&** sign, here, the process doesn't read input from a user until it's moved to the foreground.

```
[root@rad-srv ~]# tar -czf home.tar.gz . &
[1] 24180
[root@rad-srv ~]# jobs
[1]+  Running              tar -czf home.tar.gz . &
[root@rad-srv ~]#
```

You can also send a process to the background by suspending it using **[Ctrl + Z]**, this will push the SIGSTOP signal to the process, thus stopping its operations; it becomes idle:

```
[root@rad-srv ~]# tar -czf home.tar.gz.
PRESSED CTRL+Z
[2]+  Stopped              tar -czf home.tar.gz .
[root@rad-srv ~]# bg
[2]+ tar -czf home.tar.gz . &
[root@rad-srv ~]# jobs
[2]+  Running              tar -czf home.tar.gz . &
[root@rad-srv ~]#
```

To continue running the above-suspended command in the background, use the bg command:

```
[root@rad-srv ~]# tar -czf home.tar.gz.
PRESSED CTRL+Z
[2]+  Stopped              tar -czf home.tar.gz .
```

```
[root@rad-srv ~]# bg
[2]+ tar -czf home.tar.gz . &
```

To send a background process to the foreground, use the fg command together with the job ID like so:

```
[root@rad-srv ~]# jobs
[1]+  Running              tar -czf home.tar.gz . &
[root@rad-srv ~]# fg %1
tar -czf home.tar.gz
```

Process States

During execution, a process changes from one state to another depending on its environment. In Linux, a process has the following possible states; Running, waiting, stopped, and zombie. **Running** means the process is either running, and it is the current process in the system, or it is ready to start running, meaning it is waiting to be assigned to one of the system's CPUs. In the **Waiting** state, the Linux process is waiting for an event to occur or for a system resource.

Furthermore, the kernel also distinguishes between two categories of waiting processes; interruptible waiting processes, which is a process that can be interrupted by signals and uninterruptible waiting processes, which always are waiting directly on hardware conditions and cannot be interrupted by any event/signal. The Stopped process state means a process has been stopped, usually by receiving a signal. For example, a process that is being debugged.

Zombie state means that a process is dead, it has been terminated, but it still has an entry in the Linux process table.

Viewing Active Processes

We have numerous Linux utilities or commands that are utilized for viewing and displaying the list of running processes on the system, the two conventional and renowned tools are **ps** and **top** commands.

The ps Command

The ps, also known as the process status command, is a Linux command-line utility employed to deliver details about the presently running system and user processes in Linux, covering their process identification numbers known as PIDs. The **ps** utility is utilized to display all processes that are currently executing and their PIDs alongside additional information conditional on supplied command-line options.

A Linux process, also called a task, is an executing occurrence of a program. The system assigns every process a unique PID.

The fundamental syntax of the ps command in Linux

```
[root@rad-srv ~]# ps [options]
```

Running the ps command without any options displays details about a collection of executing and functional processes on the system as illustrated below:

```
[root@rad-srv ~]# ps
  PID TTY          TIME CMD
20696 pts/0    00:00:00 bash
```

```
24862 pts/0          00:00:00 ps
[root@rad-srv ~]# ps -e | head
  PID TTY          TIME CMD
    1 ?           00:00:16 init
    2 ?           00:00:00 migration/0
    3 ?           00:00:08 ksoftirqd/0
    4 ?           00:00:00 watchdog/0
    5 ?           00:00:00 events/0
    6 ?           00:00:00 khelper
    7 ?           00:00:00 kthread
   10 ?           00:00:35 kblockd/0
   11 ?           00:00:00 kacpid
[root@rad-srv ~]#
```

The output from the ps command above includes four columns of data, which are PID, TTY, TIME and CMD. PID is the process identifier, which is a distinctive number unique to a particular process. The TTY column details the user logged in a terminal type, while the TIME column records the amount of time the process has been executing in minutes and seconds, and lastly, the CMD column keeps details about the command that initialized the process.

Please note that Occasionally, the ps output may show TIME as 00:00:00 when executing the ps utility. For any process, it is nothing but the highest cumulative CPU consumption time and 00:00:00 time is an indicator that the Linux kernel has not provided any CPU time so far. In the illustration above, we notice that no CPU time is allocated for bash. Since bash is just a parent process for different processes, and bash itself does not use any CPU time up to now.

Process Viewing: To see a display of every executing process on your system use either of the two commands here: **ps –A or ps -e**

```
[root@rad-srv ~]# ps -A
 PID TTY        TIME CMD
   1 ?      00:00:16 init
   2 ?      00:00:00 migration/0
   3 ?      00:00:08 ksoftirqd/0
   4 ?      00:00:00 watchdog/0
   5 ?      00:00:00 events/0
   6 ?      00:00:00 khelper
   7 ?      00:00:00 kthread
  10 ?      00:00:35 kblockd/0
  11 ?      00:00:00 kacpid
  71 ?      00:00:00 cqueue/0
  74 ?      00:00:00 khubd
  76 ?      00:00:00 kseriod
 135 ?      00:00:00 khungtaskd
 138 ?      00:01:03 kswapd0
 139 ?      00:00:00 aio/0
 300 ?      00:00:00 kpsmoused
 323 ?      00:00:00 ata/0
 324 ?      00:00:00 ata_aux
 329 ?      00:00:00 kstriped
 338 ?      00:00:00 ksnapd
 349 ?      00:08:04 kjournald
```

375 ?	00:00:06 kauditd
408 ?	00:00:00 udevd
1297 ?	00:00:00 kmpathd/0
1298 ?	00:00:00 kmpath_handlerd
1319 ?	00:00:00 kjournald
1530 ?	00:00:00 iscsi_eh
1577 ?	00:00:00 ib_addr
1584 ?	00:00:00 ib_mcast
1585 ?	00:00:00 ib_inform
1586 ?	00:00:00 local_sa

```
[root@rad-srv ~]# ps -e
PID TTY        TIME CMD
  1 ?      00:00:16 init
  2 ?      00:00:00 migration/0
  3 ?      00:00:08 ksoftirqd/0
  4 ?      00:00:00 watchdog/0
  5 ?      00:00:00 events/0
  6 ?      00:00:00 khelper
  7 ?      00:00:00 kthread
 10 ?      00:00:35 kblockd/0
 11 ?      00:00:00 kacpid
 71 ?      00:00:00 cqueue/0
 74 ?      00:00:00 khubd
 76 ?      00:00:00 kseriod
135 ?      00:00:00 khungtaskd
138 ?      00:01:03 kswapd0
```

```
139 ?      00:00:00 aio/0
300 ?      00:00:00 kpsmoused
323 ?      00:00:00 ata/0
324 ?      00:00:00 ata_aux
329 ?      00:00:00 kstriped
338 ?      00:00:00 ksnapd
349 ?      00:08:04 kjournald
375 ?      00:00:06 kauditd
408 ?      00:00:00 udevd
1297 ?     00:00:00 kmpathd/0
1298 ?     00:00:00 kmpath_handlerd
1319 ?     00:00:00 kjournald
1530 ?     00:00:00 iscsi_eh
1577 ?     00:00:00 ib_addr
1584 ?     00:00:00 ib_mcast
1585 ?     00:00:00 ib_inform
1586 ?     00:00:00 local_sa
```

Viewing Processes not Linked to Terminal: We can see a display of all processes not associated with a terminal.

```
[root@rad-srv ~]# ps -a
 PID TTY       TIME CMD
30055 pts/0    00:00:00 ps
[root@rad-srv ~]#
```

Linux Top Utility

The Linux top utility permits system administrators and regular Linux system users to observe system and user tasks known as

135

processes and the ensuing Linux system resource usage. Top is among the principal handy utilities in the Linux system administrator's toolbox. The top command comes pre-packaged on every Linux distribution. This top command is an interactive utility or tool, which means that users can surf across the displayed process list, terminate a process, among others.

The top tool is the most fundamental commands to monitor Linux processes. It can show us an overview of the process's data and a description of the activities that the Linux kernel handles. The top command returns a listing of processes with numerous columns with details such as process name, pid, user, CPU usage and memory usages. The top command also delivers brief insights on daily machine load, use of CPU, and ram usage. Top is an essential tool for observing the use of the Linux system resources such as CPU and RAM in addition to altering the performance of the system. This section of the book will detail the various unique switches existing that can be utilized with the top command.

Typing the command top in the terminal starts an interactive terminal, as shown below.

The top part of the top command output includes process statistics and usage of system resources, whereas the bottom half consists of a catalog of the presently running Linux processes. Users can play with the arrow keys and the Page Up and Page Down keys to glance across the catalog of processes and information. Pressing the keyboard key **q quits the interactive top terminal.**

```
[root@rad-srv ~]# top
```

top - 10:27:22 up 17 days, 1:15, 1 user, load average: 0.57, 0.69, 0.68

Tasks: 150 total, 1 running, 149 sleeping, 0 stopped, 0 zombie

Cpu(s): 25.9%us, 7.6%sy, 0.0%ni, 61.8%id, 0.0%wa, 1.0%hi, 3.7%si, 0.0%st

Mem: 514432k total, 474320k used, 40112k free, 15412k buffers

Swap: 1048568k total, 140476k used, 908092k free, 284940k cached

PID	USER	PR	NI	VIRT	RES	SHR	S	%CPU	%MEM	TIME+	COMMAND
11407	named	25	0	132m	96m	1864	S	34.9	19.2	230:14.99	named
28456	postfix	15	0	7456	2520	2000	S	0.7	0.5	0:00.66	rad-srvd
10745	root	15	0	7000	1104	1004	S	0.3	0.2	7:51.99	master
1	root	15	0	2172	496	472	S	0.0	0.1	0:16.45	init
2	root	RT	-5	0	0	0	S	0.0	0.0	0:00.00	migration/0
3	root	34	19	0	0	0	S	0.0	0.0	0:08.82	ksoftirqd/0
4	root	RT	-5	0	0	0	S	0.0	0.0	0:00.00	watchdog/0
5	root	10	-5	0	0	0	S	0.0	0.0	0:00.67	events/0
6	root	12	-5	0	0	0	S	0.0	0.0	0:00.00	khelper
7	root	10	-5	0	0	0	S	0.0	0.0	0:00.00	kthread
10	root	10	-5	0	0	0	S	0.0	0.0	0:35.24	kblockd/0
11	root	20	-5	0	0	0	S	0.0	0.0	0:00.00	kacpid
71	root	19	-5	0	0	0	S	0.0	0.0	0:00.00	cqueue/0
74	root	10	-5	0	0	0	S	0.0	0.0	0:00.00	khubd
76	root	10	-5	0	0	0	S	0.0	0.0	0:00.00	kseriod
135	root	18	0	0	0	0	S	0.0	0.0	0:00.05	khungtaskd
138	root	10	-5	0	0	0	S	0.0	0.0	1:03.79	kswapd0
139	root	20	-5	0	0	0	S	0.0	0.0	0:00.00	aio/0
300	root	11	-5	0	0	0	S	0.0	0.0	0:00.00	kpsmoused

```
310 postfix  18  0  7228 2356 1932 S  0.0  0.5  0:00.01 rad-srv
321 postfix  17  0  7228 2332 1916 S  0.0  0.5  0:00.03 rad-srv
323 root     16 -5   0    0    0 S  0.0  0.0  0:00.00 ata/0
324 root     16 -5   0    0    0 S  0.0  0.0  0:00.00 ata_aux
329 root     18 -5   0    0    0 S  0.0  0.0  0:00.00 kstriped
334 postfix  18  0  7228 2360 1940 S  0.0  0.5  0:00.01 rad-srv
337 postfix  15  0  7228 2336 1916 S  0.0  0.5  0:00.00 rad-srv
338 root     20 -5   0    0    0 S  0.0  0.0  0:00.00 ksnapd
349 root     18 -5   0    0    0 S  0.0  0.0  8:05.50 kjournald
```

Reviewing Top Interface

Top command's output is split into different segments. In this book's section, we will be focusing on system load, CPU statistics, system uptime, and tasks section.

Time and Session

```
top - 20:46:05 up 5 days, 11:12,  1 user,  load average: 0.37, 0.60, 0.63
Tasks: 159 total,  2 running, 157 sleeping,  0 stopped,  0 zombie
Cpu(s): 26.9%us,  7.3%sy,  0.0%ni, 59.1%id,  0.3%wa,  1.3%hi, 5.0%si, 0.0%st
Mem:    514432k total,   478600k used,    35832k free,    13820k buffers
Swap: 1048568k total,   133508k used,   915060k free,   269380k cached

 PID USER    PR NI VIRT RES SHR S %CPU %MEM   TIME+ COMMAND
14339 named    25  0 150m 114m 1876 S 35.8 22.8 563:46.49 named
```

```
28442 root    15  0 2440 1052  796 R 0.3  0.2  0:00.04 top
28477 root    15  0 8908 2760 2224 S 0.3  0.5  0:00.01 sshd
28479 root    16  0 8616 2416 1964 S 0.3  0.5  0:00.01 sshd
28480 sshd    16  0 8616 1268  836 S 0.3  0.2  0:00.01 sshd
```

Looking at the top output results section shown above in the green shaded area we see display of the current system time which is 20:46:05, and then we see time period representing system uptime, which is the time period the Server has been running, which is 5 days 11 hours and 12 minutes as per output.

The next column of the output is showing currently active user sessions. In our top output above, there is only one active user session.

The first row of the top output also displays the system load average.

Memory and Swap Portion

```
top - 20:46:05 up 5 days, 11:12,  1 user,  load average: 0.37, 0.60,
0.63
Tasks: 159 total,  2 running, 157 sleeping,  0 stopped,  0 zombie
Cpu(s): 26.9%us,  7.3%sy,  0.0%ni, 59.1%id,  0.3%wa,  1.3%hi,
5.0%si, 0.0%st
Mem:    514432k total,   478600k used,   35832k free,    13820k
buffers
Swap: 1048568k total,   133508k used,  915060k free,   269380k
cached

 PID USER    PR NI VIRT RES SHR S %CPU %MEM   TIME+
COMMAND
```

```
14339 named    25  0  150m 114m 1876 S 35.8 22.8 563:46.49
named
28442 root   15  0  2440 1052  796 R 0.3 0.2  0:00.04 top
28477 root   15  0  8908 2760 2224 S 0.3 0.5  0:00.01 sshd
28479 root   16  0  8616 2416 1964 S 0.3 0.5  0:00.01 sshd
28480 sshd   16  0  8616 1268  836 S 0.3 0.2  0:00.01 sshd
```

The **memory and swap** part of the top results shown above in green shade displays statistics regarding the usage of swap and system memory, also known as RAM. Essentially a swap partition is a sector of the hard disk that is used as an extension of RAM. Swap partition is used when the system runs out of volatile memory. Accessing files stored on hard disk drives is relatively time-consuming, which makes usage of swap uneconomical with poor performance.

The top output in green is showing MEM values such as **total,** which denotes the total RAM size, and then we have the **free** value, which stands for the unused or available size of volatile memory. And lastly, the **used** value, which details the amount of RAM that is in use by the system.

Task Statistics

```
top - 20:46:05 up 5 days, 11:12,  1 user,  load average: 0.37, 0.60, 0.63
Tasks: 159 total,  2 running, 157 sleeping,  0 stopped,  0 zombie
Cpu(s): 26.9%us,  7.3%sy,  0.0%ni, 59.1%id,  0.3%wa,  1.3%hi, 5.0%si,  0.0%st
Mem:    514432k total,   478600k used,   35832k free,   13820k buffers
```

Swap: 1048568k total, 133508k used, 915060k free, 269380k cached

```
 PID USER    PR NI VIRT RES SHR S %CPU %MEM  TIME+
COMMAND
14339 named    25  0 150m 114m 1876 S 35.8 22.8 563:46.49
named
28442 root   15  0 2440 1052 796 R 0.3 0.2 0:00.04 top
28477 root   15  0 8908 2760 2224 S 0.3 0.5 0:00.01 sshd
28479 root   16  0 8616 2416 1964 S 0.3 0.5 0:00.01 sshd
28480 sshd   16  0 8616 1268 836 S 0.3 0.2 0:00.01 sshd
```

The output above shows the Tasks section which displays Process states and the number of tasks in that particular state. The total from the section shows the aggregate number of Tasks that are in the system. The tasks section above shows that we have 159 Tasks in total. We also have 2 Tasks that are currently in the running state, and then the remaining 157 Tasks are in the sleeping state.

CPU Statistics

```
top - 20:46:05 up 5 days, 11:12, 1 user, load average: 0.37, 0.60,
0.63
Tasks: 159 total, 2 running, 157 sleeping, 0 stopped, 0 zombie
Cpu(s): 26.9%us, 7.3%sy, 0.0%ni, 59.1%id, 0.3%wa, 1.3%hi,
5.0%si, 0.0%st
Mem:    514432k total, 478600k used,  35832k free,  13820k
buffers
Swap: 1048568k total, 133508k used, 915060k free, 269380k
cached
```

PID USER	PR	NI	VIRT	RES	SHR	S	%CPU	%MEM	TIME+
COMMAND									
14339 named	25	0	150m	114m	1876	S	35.8	22.8	563:46.49
named									
28442 root	15	0	2440	1052	796	R	0.3	0.2	0:00.04 top
28477 root	15	0	8908	2760	2224	S	0.3	0.5	0:00.01 sshd
28479 root	16	0	8616	2416	1964	S	0.3	0.5	0:00.01 sshd
28480 sshd	16	0	8616	1268	836	S	0.3	0.2	0:00.01 sshd

The green shaded area above shows CPU or processor usage statistics. This section is a display of the percentage of CPU time applied to various System tasks. The **us** percentage is displaying 26.9%, which is the percentage of CPU used to process stuff in the user space of the operating system. Comparably, the **sy percentage** value is showing that 7.3% of the CPU is used to process kernel level or system tasks in the operating system.

We also have the nice value denoted by **ni** above, which a value used to establish process priority. Processes with a higher nice value mean that they have lower priority. Similarly, Linux processes that have lower nice value means they have higher priority. The **ni** value in the top command's output results displays the proportion of time expended on running processes that have the nice value fixed manually.

The **id percentage displays the CPU** proportion of time in percent spent by the CPU doing nothing. The id above is 59.1% of the CPU. Most innovative systems switch the CPU to the energy preservation mode when they are idle or processing nothing.

The next statistic is the **wa percentage** value, which is the proportion of time in percentage that the CPU spends waiting for the processing of Input/output to conclude or finish.

Most establishments that have virtualized environment confront situations where the CPU system resources are allotted to all virtual machines. The **st value is also known as the steal time, shows the** percentage of time lost when CPU is not able to process anything due to virtual machines.

LOAD Statistics

```
top - 10:27:22 up 17 days, 1:15, 1 user, [load average: 0.57, 0.69, 0.68]
Tasks: 150 total, 1 running, 149 sleeping, 0 stopped, 0 zombie
Cpu(s): 25.9%us, 7.6%sy, 0.0%ni, 61.8%id, 0.0%wa, 1.0%hi, 3.7%si,
```

The part of the top results labeled in red and bold is the load average portion, which represents the system's average load over **one**, **five** and **fifteen** minutes. "Load" is a gauge of the volume of CPU processing effort a system implements. In the Linux operating system, the system load is the total number of processes in the runnable represented by **R** and Uninterruptible sleep symbolized by **D** states anytime. The load average value provides you a comparative measure of how prolonged you should await for CPU processing to get completed.

On a single-core architecture, the load average of 0.6 means the system is doing only 60% of the work it is meant to handle. Having a load average figure of 1 shows that the system is precisely at full capacity or is at 100%, meaning there will be overloading on the system if we add a slight fragment of extra work. Linux system that has load average of 3.42 is overloaded by 242%.

With multi-core architectures, we initially divide the load average by the sum of CPU cores to come up with a similar measure. It is noteworthy that the system load average is not our familiar standard average. We have what is called the exponential moving average, which means a little portion of the preceding load averages are factored into the present value.

Understanding the Task Area

The summary part of the top command output is comparatively easier to understand, and it includes a listing of system and user processes. In this section of the book, we are going to dive deep into the distinctive top command columns shown in the top's default output.

```
top - 17:32:26 up 17 days,  8:20,  1 user,  load average: 0.36, 0.45,
0.48
Tasks: 173 total,  1 running, 172 sleeping,  0 stopped,  0 zombie
Cpu(s): 17.2%us,  6.0%sy,  0.0%ni, 72.8%id,  0.0%wa,  0.7%hi,
3.3%si, 0.0%st
Mem:    514432k total,   503096k used,   11336k free,    22560k
buffers
Swap: 1048568k total,   140432k used,   908136k free,   281932k
cached

 PID USER    PR NI VIRT RES SHR S %CPU %MEM   TIME+
COMMAND
```

```
11407 named     25   0   147m  110m  1944 S  24.9 22.1  385:59.25
named
31239 root   15  0  2440 1056  796 R  0.7 0.2  0:00.06 top
   1 root   15  0  2172  496  472 S  0.0 0.1  0:16.72 init
   2 root   RT -5   0    0    0 S  0.0 0.0  0:00.00 migration/0
   3 root   34 19   0    0    0 S  0.0 0.0  0:09.15 ksoftirqd/0
   4 root   RT -5   0    0    0 S  0.0 0.0  0:00.00 watchdog/0
   5 root   10 -5   0    0    0 S  0.0 0.0  0:00.69 events/0
   6 root   12 -5   0    0    0 S  0.0 0.0  0:00.00 khelper
   7 root   10 -5   0    0    0 S  0.0 0.0  0:00.00 kthread
  10 root   10 -5   0    0    0 S  0.0 0.0  0:35.77 kblockd/0
  11 root   20 -5   0    0    0 S  0.0 0.0  0:00.00 kacpid
  71 root   19 -5   0    0    0 S  0.0 0.0  0:00.00 cqueue/0
  74 root   10 -5   0    0    0 S  0.0 0.0  0:00.00 khubd
  76 root   10 -5   0    0    0 S  0.0 0.0  0:00.00 kseriod
 135 root   21  0   0    0    0 S  0.0 0.0  0:00.05 khungtaskd
 138 root   10 -5   0    0    0 S  0.0 0.0  1:04.30 kswapd0
 139 root   20 -5   0    0    0 S  0.0 0.0  0:00.00 aio/0
 300 root   11 -5   0    0    0 S  0.0 0.0  0:00.00 kpsmoused
 323 root   16 -5   0    0    0 S  0.0 0.0  0:00.00 ata/0
 324 root   16 -5   0    0    0 S  0.0 0.0  0:00.00 ata_aux
 329 root   18 -5   0    0    0 S  0.0 0.0  0:00.00 kstriped
 338 root   20 -5   0    0    0 S  0.0 0.0  0:00.00 ksnapd
 349 root   10 -5   0    0    0 S  0.0 0.0  8:12.51 kjournald
 375 root   15 -5   0    0    0 S  0.0 0.0  0:06.16 kauditd
 408 root   18 -4  2408  340  336 S  0.0 0.1  0:00.45 udevd
1297 root   20 -5   0    0    0 S  0.0 0.0  0:00.00 kmpathd/0
1298 root   20 -5   0    0    0 S  0.0 0.0  0:00.00 kmpath_handlerd
1319 root   11 -5   0    0    0 S  0.0 0.0  0:00.00 kjournald
1530 root   12 -5   0    0    0 S  0.0 0.0  0:00.00 iscsi_eh
1577 root   10 -5   0    0    0 S  0.0 0.0  0:00.00 ib_addr
```

```
1584 root    12 -5   0   0   0 S 0.0 0.0  0:00.00 ib_mcast
1585 root    12 -5   0   0   0 S 0.0 0.0  0:00.00 ib_inform
1586 root    12 -5   0   0   0 S 0.0 0.0  0:00.00 local_sa
1589 root    12 -5   0   0   0 S 0.0 0.0  0:00.00 iw_cm_wq
1592 root    12 -5   0   0   0 S 0.0 0.0  0:00.00 ib_cm/0
1595 root    12 -5   0   0   0 S 0.0 0.0  0:00.00 rdma_cm
1610 root       18   0 22472  264  260 S  0.0  0.1   0:00.00
brcm_iscsiuio
1615 root    18  0 3712  356  332 S 0.0 0.1  0:02.43 iscsid
1616 root     5 -10 4168 4164 3164 S 0.0 0.8  0:00.01 iscsid
2009t    16 -4 12656  676  528 S 0.0 0.1  2:31.30 auditd
```

We have twelve columns in the process section of the default top command output, namely, **PID**, **USER**, **PR**, **NI**, **VIRT**, **RES**, **SHR**, **S**, **%CPU**, **%MEM**, **TIME+,** and **COMMAND**. We are going to detail all these columns in the ensuing section of the book. The column PID stands for process ID, which is a distinctive positive number that uniquely labels a process. The next column is the USER column, which is the operational username that incidentally maps to a filesystem user ID of the person who initiated the process. Linux allocates a genuine user ID and an operative user ID to Linux processes; the latter permits processes to perform in the stead of the other user. For instance, a regular user may elevate to a superuser like root to install some packages.

The columns **PR and NI** display the planning priority of the process from the kernel perspective, and the NI field displays the process's nice value. The process of nice value affects the process's priority.   The **VIRT, RES, SHR and %MEM fields are associated with process memory consumption.** The **VIRT** field

146

shows the total volume of memory expended by a process. This comprises the program's code, the data saved by the process in system memory, as well as any sections of memory that have been swapped to the disk. The RES field is the memory consumed by the process in RAM, and the %MEM field conveys this value as a percentage of the total RAM available. Conclusively, the SHR field is the volume of system memory jointly used with other processes. The **S field** displays the Linux process states in their single-letter mold. The **TIME+ field represents** the total CPU time expended by the process from its inception accurately to the hundredth of a second. Lastly, the **COMMAND field** displays the name or designation of the actual process.

Top Command Illustrations

The Linux top command is a utility can be. However, it can also manage processes, and you can control various aspects of top's output. In this section, we're going to take a look at a few examples.

In the illustrations underneath, the user is expected to press a key on the keyboard while the top command is still running to interact with the utility. Please note that all these key presses are case dependent as they respect lowercase and uppercase letters.

Terminating a Process

Terminating or killing a process requires the user to press 'k' on their keyboard while command top is running. The keypress results in a prompt that requests the process ID of the process you desire to kill and press enter. The line in red below shows the prompt, and in the prompt, i entered the PID 11407 of process named

```
top - 20:41:25 up 17 days, 11:29,  1 user,  load average: 0.31, 0.41,
0.43
Tasks: 214 total,  1 running, 213 sleeping,  0 stopped,  0 zombie
Cpu(s): 16.6%us,  5.0%sy,  0.0%ni, 74.8%id,  0.0%wa,  1.0%hi,
2.6%si,  0.0%st
Mem:    514432k total,   501076k used,    13356k free,    20276k
buffers
Swap: 1048568k total,   140416k used,   908152k free,   267292k
cached
PID to kill: 11407
 PID USER    PR NI VIRT RES SHR S %CPU %MEM   TIME+
COMMAND
11407 named     25   0  146m 110m 1944 S 22.9 22.0 437:08.54
named
31239 root    15  0 2440 1116  796 R  0.7 0.2  0:37.35 top
10108 postfix  16  0 7184 2164 1772 S  0.3 0.4  0:00.10 cleanup
10745 root    15  0 7000 1104 1004 S  0.3 0.2  8:05.89 master
12388 postfix  15  0 7336 2440 1984 S  0.3 0.5  0:00.01 rad-srvd
   1 root    15  0 2172 496 472 S 0.0 0.1  0:16.84 init
   2 root    RT -5   0   0   0 S 0.0 0.0  0:00.00 migration/0
```

After pressing enter above an additional prompt comes up as shown below by the red line.

```
top - 20:41:25 up 17 days, 11:29,  1 user,  load average: 0.31, 0.41,
0.43
Tasks: 214 total,  1 running, 213 sleeping,  0 stopped,  0 zombie
```

```
Cpu(s): 16.6%us,  5.0%sy,  0.0%ni, 74.8%id,  0.0%wa,  1.0%hi,
2.6%si, 0.0%st
Mem:     514432k total,   501076k used,    13356k free,    20276k
buffers
Swap: 1048568k total,   140416k used,   908152k free,   267292k
cached
Kill PID 11407 with signal [15]:
 PID USER     PR NI VIRT RES SHR S %CPU %MEM   TIME+
COMMAND
11407 named     25   0   146m 110m 1944 S 22.9 22.0 437:08.54
named
31239 root    15   0 2440 1116  796 R  0.7 0.2  0:37.35 top
10108 postfix  16   0 7184 2164 1772 S  0.3 0.4  0:00.10 cleanup
10745 root    15   0 7000 1104 1004 S  0.3 0.2  8:05.89 master
12388 postfix  15   0 7336 2440 1984 S  0.3 0.5  0:00.01 rad-srvd
 1 root    15   0 2172  496  472 S  0.0 0.1  0:16.84 init
```

The ensuing step is to enter the signal, and in the example above, the suggested signal for the process is 15. Top process uses a SIGTERM by default if the user does not enter the signal on the prompt, which permits the process earmarked for termination to die gracefully. We can use the SIGKILL to terminate a Linux process forcefully. In the top command prompt, we can type in the signal number. For instance, the signal number for the SIGTERM utility is 15, and the signal number for SIGKILL is 9.

When the user leaves an empty process ID, and presses enter, this will stop the process listed in the uppermost position on the list. Within the top output, it is possible to scroll up and down using keyboard arrow keys and alter the process you want to kill.

Sorting Processes

The most typical reason for using the top utility is to discover which process is using the most system resources. We can use the following keys to arrange the list of processes by resource usage. We use the key **M** to sort the processes by memory usage, and we use the key **P** to sort the processes by CPU usage. The other key **N** is used to sort our processes in the list by process ID. We lastly used the T key to arrange the processes by running time.

The top command shows all outcomes in a downward order by default. Nevertheless, we can toggle from the descending order to the ascending through pressing the **R** key.

It is also possible to arrange the list of processes by using the -o option or switch. For instance, when we desire to categorize processes by CPU usage, we type the following command:

ppeters@rad-srv:~$ top -o %CPU

top - 21:57:29 up 17 days, 12:42, 1 user, load average: 0.19, 0.18, 0.15

Tasks: 209 total, 2 running, 206 sleeping, 0 stopped, 1 zombie

%Cpu(s): 2.1 us, 0.2 sy, 0.0 ni, 97.7 id, 0.0 wa, 0.0 hi, 0.0 si, 0.0 st

KiB Mem: 33017660 total, 21851644 used, 11166016 free, 306668 buffers

KiB Swap: 12695347+total, 42664 used, 12691080+free. 20679308 cached Mem

PID USER   PR NI   VIRT   RES   SHR S %CPU %MEM TIME+ COMMAND

20977	www-data	20	0	475728	25252	17372	S	30.2	0.1	0:01.22	apache2
20949	www-data	20	0	471512	20844	16764	S	1.0	0.1	0:00.21	apache2
20965	www-data	20	0	472800	21292	15964	R	1.0	0.1	0:00.10	apache2
20967	www-data	20	0	473536	21340	15676	S	1.0	0.1	0:00.14	apache2
20987	www-data	20	0	472788	21420	16124	S	1.0	0.1	0:00.04	apache2
20988	www-data	20	0	473028	21208	15900	S	1.0	0.1	0:00.10	apache2
20966	www-data	20	0	0	0	0	Z	0.3	0.0	0:00.04	apache2

Listing Threads

We've also written about how Linux transitions between processes. Sadly, systems do not share storage or other assets, rendering such transitions very sluggish. Linux supports a' lightweight' variant, known as' thread.' Threads are a part of the Linux process, and they share certain storage sections and other assets, and they can be run at the same time as processes.

The top utility displays a listing of all Linux processes by default in its results. If you want to display the threads alternatively, you are required to push the H key on your keyboard while the top command is still working. Remember that the "Tasks" row instead says "Threads," which shows the amount of threads instead of the operation.

```
top - 22:10:31 up 17 days, 12:55,  1 user,  load average: 0.08, 0.11,
0.15
Threads: 214 total,  1 running, 213 sleeping,  0 stopped,  0 zombie
%Cpu(s):  0.4 us,  0.1 sy,  0.0 ni, 99.5 id,  0.0 wa,  0.0 hi,  0.0 si,  0.0
st
KiB Mem:  33017660 total, 21947456 used, 11070204 free,  306928
buffers
KiB Swap: 12695347+total,   42664 used, 12691080+free. 20742484
cached Mem

 PID USER      PR NI    VIRT    RES    SHR S %CPU %MEM
TIME+ COMMAND
21387 www-data  20   0  473104  23420  18012 S  1.7  0.1   0:00.36
apache2
21402 www-data  20   0  472812  22020  16668 S  1.3  0.1   0:00.14
apache2
21415 root      20   0  81352   5860   5024 S  1.0  0.0   0:00.03 sshd
```

From the result above, it is noticeable that the other elements in the process list did not change when we pressed the H key. This is all because the three elements namely kernel, processes, and threads, are all controlled using the uniform data structures. Accordingly, each thread in Linux is identified by a thread ID, state, etc.

We can move back to the default process view, through pushing the key 'H' again. Furthermore, we use the **-H** option or switch to show threads by default.

```
ppeters@rad-srv:~$ top -H
```

Showing Full Paths

The Linux top command does not display the Linux program or command's absolute path and does not distinguish between kernelspace and userspace programs. To get the extra details of the full path to the command, we press the key **c** while our top utility is still running. Press 'c' again to go back to the default.

```
top - 22:27:02 up 17 days, 13:12,  1 user,  load average: 0.09, 0.13,
0.13
Tasks: 208 total,  1 running, 207 sleeping,  0 stopped,  0 zombie
%Cpu(s):  0.2 us,  0.1 sy,  0.0 ni, 99.8 id,  0.0 wa,  0.0 hi,  0.0 si,  0.0
st
KiB Mem:  33017660 total, 21919504 used, 11098156 free,   307100
buffers
KiB Swap: 12695347+total,   42664 used, 12691080+free. 20741316
cached Mem

 PID USER      PR  NI   VIRT    RES    SHR S %CPU %MEM
TIME+ COMMAND
21941 www-data 20  0  473288  21116  15676 S  1.7 0.1  0:00.19
/usr/sbin/apache2 -k start
   8 root     20  0    0      0      0 S  0.3 0.0 30:28.00 [rcu_sched]
 9880 root     20  0  123308  75564  73168 S  0.3 0.2 47:28.85
/lib/systemd/systemd-journald
```

In Linux, Kernelspace, or system, processes are enclosed in square brackets. To illustrate, in the above output, we have a kernel process [rcu_sched]. To get the same output as above, we can alternatively type the example command below with the **-c** switch:

```
ppeters@rad-srv:~$ top -c
```

153

Process Forest View

Occasionally, users may desire to view the processes' child to parent hierarchy. We may achieve this by pushing either **v or V** keys while top is executing.

```
top - 22:35:50 up 17 days, 13:21,  1 user,  load average: 0.20, 0.19,
0.15
Tasks: 204 total,  1 running, 203 sleeping,  0 stopped,  0 zombie
%Cpu(s):  0.0 us,  0.0 sy,  0.0 ni, 99.9 id,  0.0 wa,  0.0 hi,  0.0 si,  0.0
st
KiB Mem:  33017660 total, 21939452 used, 11078208 free,   307152
buffers
KiB Swap: 12695347+total,    42664 used, 12691080+free. 20778596
cached Mem
```

PID USER	PR	NI	VIRT	RES	SHR	S	%CPU	%MEM	TIME+ COMMAND
1 root	20	0	28628	4068	2644	S	0.0	0.0	9:25.48 systemd
273 root	20	0	41896	2080	2076	S	0.0	0.0	0:00.54 `- systemd-udevd
570 root	20	0	37152	2816	2296	S	0.0	0.0	1:48.73 `- rpcbind
579 statd	20	0	37268	2228	2156	S	0.0	0.0	0:00.00 `- rpc.statd
593 root	20	0	23348	8	0	S	0.0	0.0	0:00.00 `- rpc.idmapd
594 daemon	20	0	19012	1540	1528	S	0.0	0.0	0:03.26 `- atd
595 root	20	0	55164	4712	4596	S	0.0	0.0	30:40.60 `- sshd

20936	root	20	0	82700	5852	5004 S	0.0	0.0	0:00.01	`-sshd
20938	ppeters	20	0	82700	3824	2980 S	0.0	0.0	0:00.45	`-sshd
20939	ppeters	20	0	22964	4824	3220 S	0.0	0.0	0:00.05	`-bash
22216	ppeters	20	0	23656	3004	2432 R	0.7	0.0	0:00.11	`-top
22174	root	20	0	55164	5324	4656 S	0.0	0.0	0:00.00	`-sshd
22182	root	20	0	55164	5344	4676 S	0.0	0.0	0:00.00	`-sshd
22206	root	20	0	55164	5208	4540 S	0.0	0.0	0:00.00	`-sshd
22207	root	20	0	55164	5468	4800 S	0.0	0.0	0:00.00	`-sshd
22210	root	20	0	55164	5456	4792 S	0.0	0.0	0:00.00	`-sshd
22215	root	20	0	55164	5488	4828 S	0.0	0.0	0:00.00	`-sshd
22217	root	20	0	55164	5436	4776 S	0.0	0.0	0:00.00	`-sshd

The top utility is immensely useful to control and handle all processes. This section of the book just scratched the surface, because there's a whole lot more we may not have addressed. For instance, there are quite numerous columns that we may add to the results of our top command. We may peruse the Linux manual pages to get more information about the columns we could add to the top command output display.

The Glances Tool

In Linux, we have a new tool called glances, which is a tool similar to top by with more advanced features. Glances has to be installed on your system.

Installing glances in CENTOS/Redhat

[root@rad-srv ~]# yum -y install glances

After installation, the glances interface is invoked by typing

[root@rad-srv ~]# glances

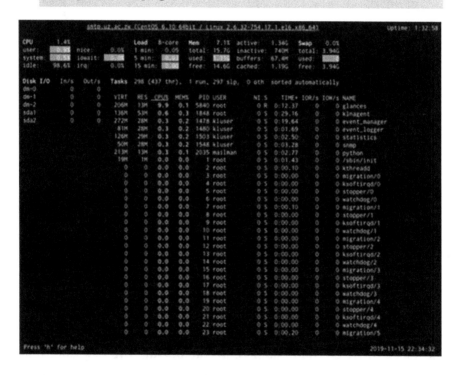

Glances – Linux Process Monitoring

Glances is a cross-platform Linux command-line utility that is based on curses and is used for system resource monitoring. Glances was developed using Python language, and the system makes use of the psutil library to take data from the Linux system. Glances enables us to monitor CPU, Load Average, Memory, Network Interfaces, Disk I/O, Processes and File System spaces utilization.

Glances is a free GPL licensed tool for the operating systems of GNU / Linux and FreeBSD. Within Glances, there are also many exciting options. One of the key features that we saw at Glances is that we can create a threshold in the configuration file (watchful, warning, and critical), and data will be displayed in colors representing the system bottlenecks.

Controlling Processes

In Linux, there are commands used for governing all processes such as kill, pkill, pgrep, and killall, below are a few basic examples of how to use them:

```
[root@rad-srv ~]# pgrep -u root top
5
8
12
16
20
24
28
32
```

```
[root@rad-srv ~]#
```

Sending Signals To Processes

The primary method of governing processes is through sending system signals to them. There are numerous system signals that may be sent to processes, and we can view all the signals through the command:

```
[root@rad-srv ~]# kill -l
 1) SIGHUP       2) SIGINT       3) SIGQUIT      4) SIGILL
 5) SIGTRAP      6) SIGABRT      7) SIGBUS       8) SIGFPE
 9) SIGKILL      10) SIGUSR1     11) SIGSEGV     12) SIGUSR2
13) SIGPIPE      14) SIGALRM     15) SIGTERM     16) SIGSTKFLT
17) SIGCHLD      18) SIGCONT     19) SIGSTOP     20) SIGTSTP
21) SIGTTIN      22) SIGTTOU     23) SIGURG      24) SIGXCPU
25) SIGXFSZ      26) SIGVTALRM   27) SIGPROF     28) SIGWINCH
29) SIGIO        30) SIGPWR      31) SIGSYS      34) SIGRTMIN
35) SIGRTMIN+1   36) SIGRTMIN+2   37) SIGRTMIN+3
38) SIGRTMIN+4   39) SIGRTMIN+5   40) SIGRTMIN+6
41) SIGRTMIN+7   42) SIGRTMIN+8   43) SIGRTMIN+9
44) SIGRTMIN+10  45) SIGRTMIN+11   46) SIGRTMIN+12
47) SIGRTMIN+13  48) SIGRTMIN+14   49) SIGRTMIN+15
50) SIGRTMAX-14  51) SIGRTMAX-13   52) SIGRTMAX-12
53) SIGRTMAX-11  54) SIGRTMAX-10   55) SIGRTMAX-9
56) SIGRTMAX-8   57) SIGRTMAX-7   58) SIGRTMAX-6
59) SIGRTMAX-5   60) SIGRTMAX-4   61) SIGRTMAX-3
62) SIGRTMAX-2   63) SIGRTMAX-1    64) SIGRTMAX
[root@rad-srv ~]#
```

To direct a signal to a Linux process, we can utilize the commands **kill**, **pkill,** and pgrep, which were stated before this. Linux programs only react to signals only if they are programmed to identify those signals.

Most kill signals in Linux are designated for system internal use only, or for use by application programmers when the program. The following are signals which are useful to a system user:

- SIGHUP 1 – this signal is sent to a process when its governing terminal is closed.

- SIGINT 2 – this signal is sent to a process by its supervisory terminal when a user interrupts the process by pressing **[Ctrl+C]**.

- SIGQUIT 3 – this signal is sent to a process if the user sends a quit signal **[Ctrl+D]**.

- SIGKILL 9 – this signal immediately ends (kills) a process, and the process will not perform any clean-up operations.

- SIGTERM 15 – this signal is an application program dissolution signal (kill will send this by default).

- SIGTSTP 20 – sent to a process by its controlling terminal to request it to stop (terminal stop), initiated by the user pressing **[Ctrl+Z]**.

The illustration below displays the kill commands example to kill the named application using its PID once it freezes:

```
[root@rad-srv ~]# pidof named
8417
[root@rad-srv ~]#
[root@rad-srv ~]# pidof named
8417
[root@rad-srv ~]# kill 8417
[root@rad-srv ~]# pidof named

[root@rad-srv ~]#
```

OR

```
[root@rad-srv ~]# pidof named
15191
[root@rad-srv ~]# kill -KILL 15191
[root@rad-srv ~]# pidof named

[root@rad-srv ~]#
```

OR

```
[root@rad-srv ~]# service named start
Starting named:                    [ OK ]
[root@rad-srv ~]# pidof named
15319
[root@rad-srv ~]# kill -SIGKILL 15319
[root@rad-srv ~]# service named status
rndc: connect failed: 127.0.0.1#953: connection refused
named dead but pid file exists
```

Changing Linux Process Priority

On the Linux system, all operational processes have a precedence and an evident nice value. Processes with higher precedence will ordinarily acquire more CPU time than inferior precedence processes.

Nevertheless, a Linux system root user can change the precedence using the nice and renice commands. From the output of the top command, the NI shows the process nice value as displayed below:

top - 17:32:26 up 17 days, 8:20, 1 user, load average: 0.36, 0.45, 0.48

Tasks: 173 total, 1 running, 172 sleeping, 0 stopped, 0 zombie

Cpu(s): 17.2%us, 6.0%sy, 0.0%ni, 72.8%id, 0.0%wa, 0.7%hi, 3.3%si, 0.0%st

Mem: 514432k total, 503096k used, 11336k free, 22560k buffers

Swap: 1048568k total, 140432k used, 908136k free, 281932k cached

PID	USER	PR	NI	VIRT	RES	SHR	S	%CPU	%MEM	TIME+	COMMAND
11407	named	25	0	147m	110m	1944	S	24.9	22.1	385:59.25	named
31239	root	15	0	2440	1056	796	R	0.7	0.2	0:00.06	top
1	root	15	0	2172	496	472	S	0.0	0.1	0:16.72	init
2	root	RT	-5	0	0	0	S	0.0	0.0	0:00.00	migration/0
3	root	34	19	0	0	0	S	0.0	0.0	0:09.15	ksoftirqd/0

4 root	RT	-5	0	0	0 S	0.0	0.0	0:00.00	watchdog/0
5 root	10	-5	0	0	0 S	0.0	0.0	0:00.69	events/0
6 root	12	-5	0	0	0 S	0.0	0.0	0:00.00	khelper
7 root	10	-5	0	0	0 S	0.0	0.0	0:00.00	kthread
10 root	10	-5	0	0	0 S	0.0	0.0	0:35.77	kblockd/0
11 root	20	-5	0	0	0 S	0.0	0.0	0:00.00	kacpid
71 root	19	-5	0	0	0 S	0.0	0.0	0:00.00	cqueue/0
74 root	10	-5	0	0	0 S	0.0	0.0	0:00.00	khubd
76 root	10	-5	0	0	0 S	0.0	0.0	0:00.00	kseriod
135 root	21	0	0	0	0 S	0.0	0.0	0:00.05	khungtaskd
138 root	10	-5	0	0	0 S	0.0	0.0	1:04.30	kswapd0
139 root	20	-5	0	0	0 S	0.0	0.0	0:00.00	aio/0
300 root	11	-5	0	0	0 S	0.0	0.0	0:00.00	kpsmoused
323 root	16	-5	0	0	0 S	0.0	0.0	0:00.00	ata/0
324 root	16	-5	0	0	0 S	0.0	0.0	0:00.00	ata_aux
329 root	18	-5	0	0	0 S	0.0	0.0	0:00.00	kstriped
338 root	20	-5	0	0	0 S	0.0	0.0	0:00.00	ksnapd
349 root	10	-5	0	0	0 S	0.0	0.0	8:12.51	kjournald
375 root	15	-5	0	0	0 S	0.0	0.0	0:06.16	kauditd
408 root	18	-4	2408	340	336 S	0.0	0.1	0:00.45	udevd
1297 root	20	-5	0	0	0 S	0.0	0.0	0:00.00	kmpathd/0
1298 root	20	-5	0	0	0 S	0.0	0.0	0:00.00	kmpath_handlerd
1319 root	11	-5	0	0	0 S	0.0	0.0	0:00.00	kjournald
1530 root	12	-5	0	0	0 S	0.0	0.0	0:00.00	iscsi_eh

List Running Processes

We utilize the nice utility to configure a nice value for Linux processes. Please note that regular users can configure only a nice value between zero and 20 to all the processes they own. In most Linux distributions, only the superuser can configure negative nice values.

To renice the precedence of a process, use the renice command as follows:

```
[root@rad-srv ~]# $ renice +9  1521
[root@rad-srv ~]# $ renice +7  1234
```

Conclusion

———•◆•———

The writer hopes that the book has managed to elevate your understanding of the Linux Command Line to the Intermediate skill level. This book covered a lot of ground in the Intermediate command-line skills. The Intermediate command line book did a preview of the "The Linux Command line" book, looking at the basic concepts of the Linux operating system, file system basics, and how to write your first bash script. The writer made deep dives into redirection, discussed file systems, disk management and logical volume management in Linux. The writer finally discussed Linux process management in finer detail and looked at the top utility used in Linux to have a glimpse of the processes running and how much system resources they are using.

The writer is going to finish the three-book series by following up with Advanced Command Line Book. Stay tuned!

www.ingramcontent.com/pod-product-compliance
Lightning Source LLC
LaVergne TN
LVHW051238050326
832903LV00028B/2456